Life Coaching for Kids

A Practical Manual to Coach Children
and Young People to Success,
Well-being and Fulfilment

Nikki Giant

Jessica Kingsley *Publishers*
London and Philadelphia

First published in 2014
by Jessica Kingsley Publishers
73 Collier Street
London N1 9BE, UK
and
400 Market Street, Suite 400
Philadelphia, PA 19106, USA

www.jkp.com

Library of Congress Cataloging in Publication Data
A CIP catalog record for this book is available from the Library of Congress

British Library Cataloguing in Publication Data
A CIP catalogue record for this book is available from the British Library

ISBN 978 1 84905 982 4
eISBN 978 0 85700 884 8

Printed and bound in Great Britain

Contents

Part 1

Exploring Life Coaching for Kids

Chapter 1

Introduction

Our children are born into the world as whole beings, perfectly innocent and ready for life's adventures. But over time, and at an increasingly faster pace, too many children become embroiled in adult problems, too often resulting in poor physical and mental health. Children are increasingly being diagnosed as anxious and depressed, developing eating disorders and addictions, labelled with behavioural problems, suffering bullying and isolation, developing low self-esteem and a poor body image and experiencing a chronic lack of self-esteem and confidence. Many of these children go unnoticed and their concerns unrecognized, such is the scale and often normalcy of today's problems.

Providing support to needy young people is often a challenge. In one classroom a teacher may be dealing with children with statements for special educational needs (SEN), young people with prominent behavioural problems, students with chronic low self-esteem or tragic home lives, and these may just be the needs of children the teacher is aware of. With an increasingly stretched curriculum, and with increasingly tight budgets, teachers, educational professionals, school counsellors, social workers and all those who support the well-being of young people are often left with a challenge – how best to support very needy children? And how best to make sure those who often sail under the radar of adults are also guided to develop socially and emotionally, as well as physically and academically?

In my role as an anti-bullying officer for a local education authority in the UK I worked with small groups of children affected by bullying, and on a one-to-one basis with a caseload of young people needing more specific support. These children and young people – of all ages – often revealed a host of complex and interconnected issues that caused or compounded the stress of bullying, or superseded it, requiring more immediate and often specialist attention. From the young woman who had taken to self-harming because of the pain of bullying she had endured, to the young man who took the stress of his parent's divorce out on other students at school, addressing each case took patience, skill, and crucially, practical strategies that the young people could connect with and understand.

School-based counselling in the UK and USA has steadily gained prominence and funding, and there is a clear place for trained counsellors experienced with working with young people in our schools, youth centres, churches and health settings. Young people are becoming more aware of a counsellor's role, and coupled with school-based efforts to promote social and emotional well-being, with time the persistent stigma around accessing mental health support will begin to subside.

But for some young people the very nature of the counselling relationship is foreign and unnatural. A one-on-one meeting with an adult may illicit fear, a presumption of wrong-doing or an immediate self-assigned label of 'there's something wrong with me'. Many excellent counsellors working with young people address these barriers every day, striving to develop a relationship of trust with their clients, and borrowing tools and ideas from a range of therapeutic approaches, including play and art therapy, cognitive behavioural therapy (CBT), life coaching, neuro-linguistic programming (NLP) and more.

In my role I felt I was becoming part counsellor-part coach, as I needed to offer both a listening ear and provide young people with practical ways to address bullying, and so it seemed sensible to integrate the two approaches. However, I felt a constant sense of limitation that any intervention provided was limited to a small number of children I could see within each school day, given the logistics of withdrawing students from class and travelling across a city from school to school. I was also becoming increasingly conscious of all those other needy young people who never came to adults' attention – those students who were bullied but never spoke up; those suffering chronic shyness and isolation each day; those who felt despair when they looked in the mirror; who had experienced domestic abuse at home; or who had no goals or sense of purpose. Although not every child is unfortunate enough to experience a debilitating physical, emotional, social or life problem, nearly every young person could benefit from a helping hand to become more confident and resilient, and to develop aspirations to be inspired by life's potential.

Life Coaching for Kids is an approach and resource to support all those young people. Borrowing principles from the life coaching process and coupled with practical tools, activities and worksheets, *Life Coaching for Kids* integrates the theory and grounding of a supportive, mentoring relationship with the practical, solution-focused tools of life coaching, specifically for children and young people. *Life Coaching for Kids* lends itself to a formal process of one-on-one support, but is equally just as useful in the home delivered by parents, in the classroom during a Personal, Social and Health Education (PSHE) lesson, or crucially, offering a method for young people to become their own best coach by using the tools independently. Please note that in order to avoid gendered stereotyping, 'he' and 'she' have been used alternatively for each chapter and theme. Also, the terms 'parent', 'carer', 'caregiver' and 'guardian' have been used interchangeably for an adult caregiver with responsibility for a young person's well-being.

Although a fairly new form of support, life coaching is a well-recognized and practical model to support people to make concrete changes in their lives. The positive, solution-focused approach of coaching is suitable for children and young people of all ages, building lifelong tools and awareness to help them maintain good mental health and to stay in charge of their well-being.

This resource has been written for the teacher, school counsellor, educational psychologist, youth worker, pastoral leader or parent (or guardian) seeking to support children and young people to build a positive outlook, to set and reach life goals, to develop confidence, and to celebrate who they are.

Life Coaching for Kids is not a substitute for thorough training in counselling, coaching or other forms of therapy, and nor are the tools designed to form a completely therapeutic process. Rather, *Life Coaching for Kids* explores the life coaching model, presenting the key strategies and processes used in coaching to be integrated into daily working practice with children and young people, or to help children feel happier at home. These tools, activities and worksheets are simple to use, practical, hands-on, and address a range of key issues young people face, from a lack of confidence, to bullying, peer pressure, friendship woes, or exam stresses.

No child should become jaded before reaching their teenage years, nor should they be labelled as a 'problem' before adulthood, nor dismissed as 'no-hopers' before they've had a chance to work out who they are and where their passions lie. With a collective effort, as parents or guardians, educators and advocates for children and young people, we can create a generation of self-aware youth, armed with the tools, knowledge and strategies to not only cope, but to thrive.

Chapter 2

What is Life Coaching?

Coaching is a broad and expansive term that encompasses a wide range of applications, theories, approaches, disciplines and client groups. The very notion of a coach will mean something different to each of us – to some, a coach conjures an immediate association with sports, while for others, a mental image of a mentor or supporter comes to mind, such as a family member or best friend.

The International Coach Federation (ICF), a worldwide professional body for coaches of all disciplines, defines coaching as the 'partnering with clients in a thought-provoking and creative process that inspires them to maximize their personal and professional potential' (ICF 2013). In the most basic sense, a coach can be described as any person who strives to support, train, instruct or mentor another towards a defined goal or outcome, such as a sports instructor or leadership coach. Within the last few decades, the term 'coaching' has growing to include a vast array of specialisms and models, from non-therapeutic support, business or executive coaching focusing on creating better outcomes in a work environment, wellness coaching to develop a client's physical or emotional well-being, and life coaching, a practical and goal-oriented intervention that will typically address personal and life-based issues related to career, family, relationships, health, and so on.

Background to life coaching

Life coaching grew from executive and leadership coaching models, gaining popularity and recognition in the 1980s.

Executive coaching is defined by *The Executive Coaching Handbook* as 'an experiential and individualized leader development process that builds a leader's capability to achieve short- and long-term organizational goals. The organization, an executive, and the executive coach work in partnership to achieve maximum impact' (TECF 2008, p.19). Executive or leadership coaches work with people from all walks of life and in a variety of businesses and industries to develop their skills and capacity to achieve business goals, motivate staff, liaise with clients, and to enable their business to function effectively and productively.

Given the success of coaching in work-related realms, coaches began to note the potential for transferring these strategies and tools to help clients make changes in their personal lives. Some executive coaches found that their clients' development was being hampered by problems at home, while for others, workplace dramas were affecting home life.

Work–life balance is a popular and well-understood term today that speaks of the importance of workers maintaining a balance between their professional and personal lives. As any person who has struggled with a life issue can attest, work and home cannot always be effectively separated. A sick child at home, a looming divorce, family bereavement – personal issues can easily impact upon a person's ability to maintain productivity and success at work. Similarly, high-stress job roles, workplace grievances, conflicts with colleagues and a whole host of anxiety-inducing professional problems will naturally impact upon family life. The tools and strategies used by executive coaches began to work for clients away from the office, and life coaching has since grown to become a popular form of support in its own right.

What is life coaching?

As the name suggests, life coaches help their clients to live more successful, happy and fulfilled lives, coaching on general well-being and/or specific issues that affect people's ability to grow, prosper and flourish. From weight and body image concerns, to bullying, addictions, financial problems, confidence issues, managing life transitions such as divorce or retirement or exploring stress management techniques, the life coaching relationship and tools can help people to identify a way forward and move towards a new life vision.

Life coaching is generally viewed as a less intensive, short-term and more practically focused form of support than counselling or psychotherapy, although coaching can also be therapeutic. Some people choose coaching over other forms of therapy because of its goal-oriented nature, as life coaching sessions will typically provide clients with specific activities, practical exercises they can use themselves and homework to continue their progress between sessions or after the coaching relationship has come to an end. For some, coaching is the solution to a specific, concrete problem, as opposed to needing help to define the problem, or looking for answers about *why* the problem exists, which may be the role of counselling or more intensive personal therapy.

As coaching is typically goal-oriented and future-focused, it is often suited to those who want to make tangible changes and/or those who do not have deep-seated issues, have experienced trauma, grief or intense depression, or have significant mental health problems *where the client wishes to address these concerns.* Coaching may not be suitable for a client who is in the depths of a deep grieving process, for example. This client might instead need the ongoing support of a trained grief counsellor to create a safe space and relationship in which to process the grief and work towards some level of acceptance. However, life coaching can still be utilized to address specific goals for a client with deep-seated issues or receiving more intensive therapy elsewhere. For example, a client suffering from severe mental health problems may wish to see a life coach (possibly alongside other forms of therapy) to work on the specific goal of becoming more organized and self-sufficient in a living situation, or working towards securing paid employment.

Life coaching is future-focused: a coach and client collaborate to set intentions and to create change for the client's future, rather than looking back at the past. Although our personal history can provide us with clues and answers as to why we are in our current life situation, and is therefore acknowledged in the coaching process, the purpose of life coaching is to move forward, rather than utilizing sessions to analyse, unpick and fix past experiences as one may do through a counselling or therapy process.

Life coaches help people to:

- set realistic goals

- create steps towards those goals

- create a space or an environment in which change can occur

- look for feedback and measure progress

- build self-awareness, self-belief, internal resources and resilience

- focus on their potential and the future

- create their own toolkit of resources and strategies to use at any time

- be empowered to plan and take steps on a path towards change, supporting people to move forward on their journey through life.

A formal life coaching relationship can be a short or long-term intervention, depending upon the client's issues and goals. Coaching can be provided face-to-face or increasingly is conducted by telephone, email or web-based video chat.

Defining and understanding life coaching

Life coaching

Life coaching can be defined as the provision of client-centred support, utilizing therapeutic and practical techniques in a teaching format, to assist a client to achieve self-defined goals and outcomes. The key elements of this definition are:

- a client-centred model

- therapeutic and practical techniques

- supporting clients' self-defined goals and outcomes.

A CLIENT-CENTRED MODEL

A client or person-centred approach is a model of support that places the client at the centre of the therapeutic relationship. This approach asserts that each client is the expert on themselves, not the counsellor or therapist. This is a contrast to psychoanalytic models of helping which define the therapist as the expert and guide for the client. While the coach may have significant training, experience, knowledge and tools to support the client, the coach will not analyse or diagnose; instead clients are encouraged to share thoughts, feelings and experiences and to be supported to understand themselves better, growing in self-awareness through the relationship with their therapist or coach. The client is the central point around which the relationship focuses, working at the client's pace and being led by the client's needs.

In coaching, being client-centred means working alongside a person to create goals and to define where change needs to be made, and how.

THERAPEUTIC AND PRACTICAL TECHNIQUES

Life coaching provides clients with a balance of practical, solution-oriented tools and strategies, and a therapeutic or safe space in which exploration, change and growth can occur. Without either element a true coaching process cannot take place. Coaching with an absence of techniques or a lack of focus on a solution traverses into the realms of, at best, a purely counselling or supportive scenario, or at worst, a well-meaning chat. Similarly, without the coach creating an environment of safety, trust, empathy and non-judgement, a client would likely feel unable or unwilling to fully share and explore issues of concern, and therefore be unable to use the tools available to any significant degree.

Practical techniques are what typically will differentiate coaching from other forms of support, such as counselling or mentoring. A coach may support a client to conduct an internet search or seek out a self-help book from the library, or use a scaling model to help identify how lacking in confidence the client really is, and where the client wants to get to. A practical tool may be a meditation script for a client to self-administer, or a breathing technique to help reduce anxiety. These practical strategies help to place a client's progress in the client's own hands and build capacity to create and maintain their own progress, as the tools can be reused at any time. The practical nature of coaching makes it a highly applicable form of support for children and young people who are typically more engaged and comfortable with hands-on and interactive support.

For children and young people, the therapeutic element of coaching is just as crucial as it is for adults. Creating a relationship and environment of safety, trust, empathy and active listening will help youth with specific issues of concern to feel confident and supported to begin to explore and address their problems. While the coaching tools can easily be used in a less formal, non-therapeutic environment, for example, in a whole-classroom setting, a balance of therapeutic and practical techniques shifts the coaching relationship from an instructive or teaching-and-learning process to a space for healing and growth to take place.

SUPPORTING CLIENTS' SELF-DEFINED GOALS AND OUTCOMES

A key feature of a person-centred coaching approach is helping clients to identify and reach their own goals. Rather than a parent, teacher or mentor telling children what they should be focusing on or how they should be living their life, a coach will help clients place their own finger upon where change needs to occur in their life, and help to find a way for those changes to occur. The coach may have some insight into how clients could move forward successfully, or where they may be holding themselves back, and so it is through collaborative exploration, with guidance, that clients will identify the outcomes they wish to achieve through coaching. This process will help clients to similarly identify and make changes in their lives post-coaching, empowering and equipping them with the process, tools and insight to continue to grow and develop in the future.

This approach may be somewhat alien to some teachers and parents who are more accustomed to setting goals and targets for children, rather than encouraging the children to do so for themselves. In a coaching scenario adults will need to relinquish a certain degree of control to let children set the agenda. As is true of both adults and children, people are more likely to be motivated to reach their goals if they are not imposed by someone else – as caring adults we must trust that children know their own minds and are aware of what needs to change for the better in their lives, with our guidance. This may be an ongoing process, however – as the coaching relationship develops, children may feel more comfortable and equipped to explore deeper goals, moving past surface issues to intrinsic change.

Additional key features of life coaching

Many models of therapeutic support borrow tools, theory and technique from one another or therapists may choose to integrate and marry theories within their practice. The following are some key features that differentiate life coaching from other forms of support. These may be specific to life coaching or also used in other forms of support, such as CBT, motivational interviewing, mentoring or person-centred counselling.

A SOLUTION-FOCUSED APPROACH

Coaching focuses on finding solutions and looking forward, rather than looking back to the past or reviewing problems. While it is useful to explore our past, and perhaps to begin to understand the roots of some of our problems, for some clients this awareness – while helpful – does not change anything in the here-and-now. For example, a client who grew up in an impoverished household with little money may, through exploration with her therapist, begin to understand that she has inherited a mindset of scarcity and lack, believing that money problems are always just around the corner or destitution will hit at any moment. Through therapy the client may understand more about how her past experiences have translated into present-day fears, and this awareness alone may help to overcome these limiting thoughts. However, for some clients this understanding is not enough to make tangible changes to the quality of their life now. A solution-focused coaching approach can help clients to manage their money, budget, set financial goals, create a wealth mindset or a financial safety net, and develop positive thinking tools when old fears about lack and scarcity creep in.

A solution-focused approach is particularly useful for children and young people who often cannot conceptualize the idea that past problems create present results, or verbalize the root of their concerns to any great degree. For example, a young person with poor self-image may not remember when she started to dislike her body or feel unconfident about her image. She may not understand the link between her current state of mind and a critical parent who often passed negative comment on her looks, for example, or the effects of a spate of bullying that led her to this unfortunate assumption about her looks. Rather, this child needs support to acknowledge her positive attributes and rebuild her confidence in the here-and-now. A focus on finding solutions is positive and practical.

UTILIZING RAPID INTERVENTIONS

Life coaches will often utilize rapid interventions with their clients to create behavioural changes and faster results than other forms of therapy or counselling. Rapid interventions are not quick fixes or magic wands, and will not work for every client. Some clients will need more intensive coaching, or to explore deep-rooted issues before any change can occur.

Rapid interventions are used to help clients define the problem or issue they wish to change, and to explore and implement new patterns of behaviour. A coach will help clients to stick to these new patterns. Rapid or brief interventions can be found in CBT, motivational counselling, hypnotherapy and other forms of support, and may require training and practice before using with a client.

FACILITATING BEHAVIOURAL CHANGE

The core aim of formal life coaching is to create positive behavioural change in clients. Coaches and clients work together to identify the thoughts, feelings and behaviours that do not serve them well, and produce a plan to create change, often utilizing rapid interventions, tools and techniques.

Creating behavioural change does not mean enforcing change upon young people's behaviour because they act in ways that we, as adults, don't like. Implementing classroom behavioural management techniques and coaching children to make behavioural changes are two very different things. In a role as coach, an adult will support a young person to identify for herself the aspects of her behaviour that would best serve her to change or positively develop, and support the child to reach this goal, so that she ultimately feels happier, healthier and more fulfilled. Facilitating behavioural change is not a punitive measure and should not be used to force children to comply, or fit in to an environment we have created. Coaching should always be a positive, supportive measure, and not a reprimand or a consequence to poor behaviour.

Life coaches do not:

- solve problems

- make 'quick fixes' or wave a magic wand

- make people change: they enable a *change process* to occur.

The myths and pitfalls of life coaching

Despite growing public awareness of the importance of promoting good mental as well as physical health, dealing with and talking about emotional problems, life issues and mental health is often still a taboo. Counselling and therapy are still too commonly viewed as something for 'them' and not 'me', and myths and misconceptions still persist. Thankfully, child and adolescent counselling is a growing field, and many schools now employ counsellors to serve the needs of students, although this is more common in secondary schools than at primary or junior school level. Children and young people are often more adept at talking about their feelings and sharing their problems than adults who have learned to maintain a 'stiff upper lip' and to hide their worries and feelings.

A report commissioned by the Welsh Government in the UK into counselling in schools (2011) found that young people were welcoming of counselling services in their schools, but shared mixed concerns about using the services. One young person stated, 'Counselling may make people more confident. I didn't want to see a [student] buddy in Year 7 – I didn't trust them. I would have liked to have seen an adult professional counsellor' (quoted in BACP 2007, p.42). The report also highlighted the barriers to counselling, including young people not knowing about the service and being seen attending counselling and therefore attracting unwanted attention or bullying.

The stigma of accessing talking therapies and trained support still persists for young people as it does for adults. Some children are worried about being labelled as having a problem if they share their concerns with a school counsellor, or are concerned that anything they say might be fed back to their teachers or parents. For other young people, counselling is viewed as being for people with 'real' problems, and they keep their concerns private. Providing life coaching to young people in formal settings such as schools may encounter the same blocks, barriers and challenges as counselling, and some schools may instead choose to utilize coaching techniques in non-formal group, one-on-one or whole-class settings, rather than establishing a formal coaching support service in school. (More information about the differences between coaching and counselling are explored in Chapter 4.)

Life coaching, as a fairly new form of support, is sometimes viewed as 'new age' and not grounded in science or theory, or is seen as being only for executives and business people, thanks to its roots in leadership coaching. For others, coaching is more appealing but is mistakenly labelled as a way to fix anything in a couple of sessions, because of the solution-focused approach and rapid or brief interventions used. This dangerous concept can lead clients who are in need of long-term therapy or professional, targeted support (such as mental health counselling or psychiatry) to access coaching believing it to be a quick-fix solution. This misguided view can also suggest that a client doesn't have to do much in coaching and that it's going to be an easy ride to fast change, which often isn't the case.

The misconceptions about coaching tools, behavioural change and rapid interventions may also lead clients to believe that coaching can 'cure' deep-seated emotional problems in an instant, without deeper contemplation or a commitment to spending the necessary time with a therapist or coach. While rapid interventions may be successful for some, each person will respond differently to the coaching tools and relationship.

Coaching is neither a quick fix nor an easy solution, neither is it a poor relation to other forms of therapy or counselling. It is a good fit for some clients and not for others – its suitability is dependent on a client's needs, issues of concern, goals and mindset.

Regulating life coaching

Coaching is typically non-regulated, meaning that practitioners aren't subject to governing codes of practice, ethical guidelines or other regulatory measures, unless they choose to be associated with a national or international professional body. This is gradually changing, and coaching and other forms of therapy are becoming more regulated in various countries around the world. In the most positive sense, non-regulation creates a large body of practitioners, coaching both formally and informally in various roles and capacities to improve the lives of their clients. Those wishing to become coaches don't need to undergo expensive and lengthy training and certification, and can grow their experience and expertise as they support clients. On the flipside, this can leave unmonitored gaps of poor practice, unethical working and poorly trained practitioners doing more harm than good.

In 2006 in the UK the Coaching and Mentoring National Occupational Standards (NOS) were developed to provide a nationally recognized and agreed set of standards for those working in coaching and mentoring roles, in order to provide guidelines for effective performance agreed by a panel of employers, stakeholders and representatives from NOS. The Standards describe 'what an individual needs to do, know and understand in order to carry out a particular job role or function', in this case, those engaged in mentoring or coaching in either a formal or informal capacity (The Coaching Academy 2011). The NOS can help both experienced and novice coaches to assess their practice and skills, ensure their continued professional development, and are increasingly used by awarding bodies and regulatory organizations to develop and approve new qualifications.

The NOS for counselling, which also apply to the practice of life coaching, provide a widely recognized and agreed-upon framework for therapists to practice ethically, safely and competently. They define the standards of good practice expected from therapists working at all levels in the field, and provide both new and experienced professionals with a benchmark with which to measure their practice and ensure that the service they are providing best meets the needs of the individual client and the industry as a whole. The NOS help to regulate the industry and bring a sense of uniformity to practice, so that clients can expect the same level of professionalism and care from any therapist they may seek to work with, despite any differing theoretical standpoint or type of counselling or coaching being offered.

When working with children and young people, in any capacity, certain protocols and practices must be followed, to keep both children and adults safe. In an increasingly litigious society adults can be wrongly accused of harming children, or more worryingly, preying adults can gain access to vulnerable children when proper safety and child protection procedures are not in place, such as background or police-checking adults who will come into contact with children and young people. Maintaining the well-being and safety of children is always paramount, particularly when addressing social, emotional or behavioural issues or sensitive life problems, such as bullying, bereavement or family difficulties. Anyone working with a child or young person in a coaching capacity should ensure they are working to an appropriate ethical framework and child protection policy.

Examples of coaching clients and goals

A vast array of people seeks support from life coaches for a variety of problems. Coaches help with deep-seated, historical problems that require therapeutic intervention as well as practical tools, and also with surface issues, obtaining goals and making behavioural changes by applying concrete strategies and taking action-oriented steps. There is no one 'type' of coaching client as the applications of coaching are so wide, but life coaching may be a solution more suited to some clients than others, and it is important that people find the right fitting support for them.

The *Life Coaching for Kids* tools are suitable for children and young people in primary and secondary school settings, to address specific issues or general well-being with young people. However, the following may provide a greater understanding of how formal life coaching can help people in a wider sense, and why clients may seek coaching support, to help clarify and ground the concept of life coaching.

Client Example One: A professional woman suffers from a lack of confidence and is finding social situations increasingly difficult. She wishes to use life coaching to help her become more confident and self-assured, particularly when speaking to people she doesn't know. Her goals centre on looking and feeling more confident, developing her public speaking and feeling more worthy of people's attention.

Client Example Two: A young man is experiencing persistent bullying in the workplace. He is fearful about speaking up and is missing an increasing number of days of work because of his fear of running into his tormentor at work. He wishes to use life coaching to become more resilient and self-assured, processing his feelings about the bullying, and coping through the process of reporting the bullying to his manager.

Client Example Three: A woman in her mid-fifties has recently divorced and is adjusting to her new single life. She wishes to use coaching to help create new goals and a new life plan now that she has the freedom to pursue an old passion of running her own business that she felt unable to explore while married. Her goals centre on defining herself as newly single, building a social life and planning steps towards starting a business.

Client Example Four: A seven-year-old boy has been having problems sleeping and is increasingly anxious at night-time. His parents have brought him to coaching to find a way to deal with the worries keeping him awake and to be able to sleep and rest more easily. His coaching goals focus on relaxation techniques and finding methods to fall asleep, while exploring and minimizing some of his worries and anxieties.

Client Example Five: A client has severe mental health problems and is in long-term counselling. She has been referred for coaching by her psychiatrist to help deal with practical life issues. Lately her schizophrenia is impacting upon her ability to maintain a clean home, to run errands and engage in social pursuits at the local community centre, and she feels lost and hopeless. She wishes to use coaching to help create a weekly plan for staying on task with her chores and social activities, while broadening her life by taking up a hobby of painting and drawing.

Coaching can assist people from all walks of life, and similarly, can support children and young people of all ages, backgrounds, ability levels and with a variety of issues and concerns. (Further exploration of potential child and adolescent issues that may benefit from coaching support can be found in Chapter 3.)

Chapter summary

- Life coaching is a client-centred model, using therapeutic and practical techniques, and supporting clients' self-defined goals and outcomes.

- Life coaching is solution-focused and facilitates behavioural change.

- Life coaches do not solve problems, make 'quick fixes' or make people change.

- Life coaching is not regulated, and differs from counselling and other forms of therapy.

Chapter 3

Why Coach Kids?

Many children growing up in the world today are richer than any generation before. Millions of children have mobile phones, computers, branded clothes, games consoles and various other trappings of 21st-century living. They have access to more information than the world's largest library at their fingertips, and are typically better educated than their parents or grandparents. So arguably, children in the UK, USA and other wealthy nations should be the happiest, healthiest and most successful on Earth. And yet, baffling stories of youth bullying, depression, suicide, disaffection, school disengagement and a whole litany of other problems seem to plague our children. Growing up has never seemed harder.

A United Nations Children's Fund (UNICEF) study on children's well-being reported that the UK ranked 16 out of 29 developed countries in 2013, although this is an improvement on last place in 2007. UNICEF ranked the 29 developed countries according to the overall well-being of their children, exploring five dimensions of well-being to give each country its overall ranking: education, health and safety, material well-being, behaviours and risks, and housing and environment. The USA, one of the richest nations on Earth, ranked 26th; only Lithuania, Latvia and Romania (three of the poorest countries in the survey) had reportedly worse levels of child well-being than the USA. Despite the common perception that a richer nation equals richer and therefore happier citizens, the research attests that there does not appear to be a strong correlation between children's well-being and a country's per capita gross domestic product (GDP).

UNICEF measured a number of factors to determine the level of children's well-being, including obesity, exposure to violence including bullying, health at birth, risky behaviours such as smoking and drug-taking, participation and achievement in school, and the child poverty and family affluence rate.

Canada and the USA were two of the three bottom nations for the percentage of children overweight by their body mass index (BMI), with obesity levels higher than 20 per cent. The UK ranked third from bottom and the USA bottom in the table of countries when measuring the teenage fertility rate, with over 29 teenage births per 1000 young women.

Following from the UK's poor ranking in 2007, a report commissioned by UNICEF UK and compiled by Ipsos MORI was released in 2011 to compare child well-being in the UK, Spain and Sweden. The research explored the reasons behind the UK's poor ranking in UNICEF's overall well-being measurement in 2007 and previous years, by comparing children's experiences in the UK with those of children in Spain and Sweden, two higher-ranking countries.

Researchers found that the well-being of children in the UK fell short of their Swedish and Spanish counterparts in many ways. Children in the UK were less likely to take part in creative and interest-based pursuits by the time they reached secondary school, despite saying these activities made them happy, and UK families reported a greater pressure to consume and be materially focused than families in Spain and Sweden. The research also found that many parents in the UK were concerned with material status and purchased goods to hide social insecurities, which was not the case in Spain and Sweden (Ipsos MORI 2011).

In the USA the Foundation for Child Development (FCD) uses social indicators to measure child well-being at federal and state levels. In 2004, the Foundation released the first Child Well-being Index (CWI), a comprehensive measure of the quality of life for children and youth. The CWI combines national data from a range of indicators across seven quality-of-life domains, including educational attainment, social relationships, family economic well-being and health factors. The most recent CWI reports that American families experienced a decade of economic decline from 2001–11, leaving more children in poverty than in 1975 (FCD 2012).

The Federal Interagency Forum on Child and Family Statistics compiled a report on child well-being in the USA. *America's Children: Key National Indicators of Well-being, 2013* explored seven key indicators to well-being, similar to those used by the FCD (2013). They reported that of the 73.7 million children and young people living in the USA:

- 22 per cent aged 0–17 (16.1 million) lived in poverty

- 24 per cent of 12th graders engaged in binge drinking in 2012 (consuming five or more alcoholic beverages in a row in the past two weeks)

- 18 per cent of children aged 6–17 were obese.

In the UK a report was commissioned by the Welsh Government (2011) into the well-being of children and young people, in response to calls from the United Nations (UN) for governments to improve outcomes for children and young people by assessing progress towards well-being measurements. In Wales:

- The number of looked-after children has increased by 44 per cent over the last decade. Looked-after children have considerably lower attainment rates than all students.

- The rate of hospital admissions for self-harm in Wales has increased in recent years and is higher for girls than for boys, particularly among 15- to 17-year-olds.

- Young people in Wales aged 16–29 were significantly more likely to be victims of discrimination, harassment or victimization than residents over 40.

These statistics are extremely concerning, and paint a worrying picture about our young people, indicating the need for emotional and mental health support to be more readily available. But it is not only significant problems that affect youth. Research conducted by the Department for Children, Schools and Families found that children aged 12–15 worried most about exams, school work and their future, as well as sex and girlfriends or boyfriends, and being healthy. Children aged 9–10 worried most about friendships, exams and being bullied (2007 DCSF).

The UK charity ChildLine received 1.5 million contacts in 2011/12, including 1.2 million phone calls. Their website received 1.85 million visits, an increase of 36 per cent from 2010/11. The top five reasons children and young people contacted the charity for support were: family relationships; bullying; physical abuse; self-harm; and sexual abuse. Children requesting help and advice about self-harm rose 68 per cent in one year from 2010/11. Calls and online requests for support about suicide increased by 39 per cent on the previous year, particularly from girls aged 16–18. Requests for help with eating problems also rose by 43 per cent (ChildLine 2012).

A similar picture is evident in the USA. The Centers for Disease Control and Prevention (CDC), a government agency protecting public health and safety, conducts and produces research on young people's health and safety across the USA. The national Youth Risk Behaviour Survey (YRBS) is conducted with young people across the USA in school grades 9–12 (ages 14 to 18). The survey monitors a range of priority health-risk behaviours that contribute markedly to the leading causes of death, disability and social problems among youth and adults in the USA. In 2011 the survey found that:

- 24 per cent of students had ridden one or more times in a car or other vehicle driven by someone who had been drinking alcohol

- 17 per cent of students had carried a weapon (for example, a gun, knife or club) on at least one day during the 30 days before the survey

- 5 per cent of students had carried a gun on at least one day during the 30 days before the survey

- 8 per cent of students had ever been physically forced to have sexual intercourse when they did not want to

- 16 per cent of students had seriously considered attempting suicide during the 12 months before the survey, of which 7.8 per cent had attempted suicide

- 26 per cent of students had been offered, sold or given an illegal drug by someone on school property during the 12 months before the survey

- 15 per cent of students had had sexual intercourse with four or more people during their life.

Efforts to improve youth well-being are crucial, and must be both preventative as well as reactive. Research conducted by The Children's Society in the UK found that children's levels of well-being can be changed and improved by external factors, and that being active, creativity, play, family time and other activities help to improve well-being. However, *The Good Childhood Report 2013* also presents worrying implications for not addressing well-being. 'Children with low well-being are over twenty times less likely than other children to feel safe at home, eight times more likely to say that their family does not get along well together and five times more likely to report having recently been bullied' (The Children's Society 2013, p.3).

Issues affecting well-being in school

As the pressure to improve children and young people's well-being increases, measures are being taken to protect and support children and families at various levels, including within national policy, local government, schools and community services. Schools are increasingly working to promote students' well-being, which may include providing PSHE or citizenship lessons on themes such as personal safety, substance misuse and relationships; protecting students from bullying; providing opportunities to engage learners in school life and to have their voice heard; or providing support services to students in need, such as access to school counselling.

The role of schools in supporting youth well-being is crucial. Children and young people are unlikely to be able to sufficiently learn, process or retain information when experiencing an issue or life circumstance that affects their health or well-being. For some students this may be an atypical or occasional problem, such as experiencing bullying or falling out with friends. For others, their well-being and general experience of life may be significantly and detrimentally affected by a recurrent problem or an ongoing fact of life that they cannot change, such as being a carer to a disabled parent or experiencing chronic low self-esteem. Providing support to all young people is a challenge, given the broad nature of concerns youth may experience through their childhood and adolescence, and the volume of young people any one teacher or school may encounter. However, given the access schools have to children and their families, and the time spent by children in education, support services and efforts to improve well-being and to develop young people's social and emotional literacy are well-placed in schools.

Educational attainment and school attendance are likely casualties of poor well-being. As children struggle with issues affecting their physical and mental health, such as bullying, parental divorce or drug addiction, their ability to actively participate in their education and remain in school is diminished. While the remit of schools is undoubtedly still to teach a curriculum and build children's knowledge, there is a place for school-based efforts to improve health and well-being.

Why use coaching with children and young people?

The problems affecting children and young people are largely universal. Issues such as bullying, substance misuse, domestic abuse, peer pressure, family problems, obesity, poor body image and more can affect youth regardless of their culture, ethnicity, religion or family background. While some issues may be more prevalent for girls than boys, or affect older youth more than younger children, there is a need to address the social and emotional well-being of all young people.

In the UK efforts to provide a more well-rounded education to young people and to develop children socially and emotionally, as well as academically, saw the introduction of programmes such as SEAL – Social and Emotional Aspects of Learning. SEAL was introduced to primary and secondary school classrooms through a curriculum exploring five themes – self-awareness, managing feelings, motivation, empathy and social skills – with the ethos of SEAL embedded throughout the school.

The SEAL curriculum highlights why social and emotional skills are important, including helping to improve academic results, encouraging better behaviour and attendance in young people and creating a more positive school ethos (DfE 2010). The SEAL programme complemented research about the importance of social and emotional literacy, reflecting Daniel Goleman's seminal books on the themes that introduced the idea of emotional intelligence (EI) being as important as IQ (intelligence quotient). Goleman highlighted how high-stress situations and emotions such as fear or anger can create a fight or flight response in the body, which becomes flooded with stress hormones. In this situation the emotional part of the brain, the amygdala (which regulates the fight or flight response), feels threatened and can 'hijack' the rational brain (Goleman 1996). The need to create peaceful, stable environments conducive to learning taking place is clear. For children in highly stressful situations, or whose social and emotional well-being is threatened or debilitated, the ability to stay calm, rational and engaged in learning (or any other situation) is limited.

Research conducted by the University of Chicago and the US-based Collaborative for Academic Social and Emotional Learning (CASEL) found that Social and Emotional Learning (SEL) programmes improve students' attitudes about self and others, connection to school, positive social behaviour, reduce conduct problems and emotional distress, and improve students' achievement test scores by 11 percentile points (Durlak *et al.* 2011).

In a 2004 book entitled *Building Academic Success on Social and Emotional Learning: What Does the Research Say?* Zins *et al.* explore why social and emotional learning is important in schools.

Intrinsically, schools are social places and learning is a social process. Students do not learn alone but rather in collaboration with their teachers, in the company of their peers, and with the support of their families. Emotions can facilitate or hamper their learning and their ultimate success in school. Because social and emotional factors play such an important role, schools must attend to this aspect of the educational process for the benefit of all students. (Zins *et al.* 2004, p.3)

There is a clear need to address children's well-being both in and outside of school, and to build the social and emotional intelligence of young people alongside their academic ability. This will help young people to become resilient, positive in the face of adversity, and most importantly, equipped with the necessary tools to cope and find support when issues and life events occur that threaten well-being.

Life coaching builds skills and awareness, helping children and young people to understand themselves better, identify issues of concern or goals they wish to reach, and develop methods for managing their emotions and improving their life situation. Although some life events and problems may be permanent or unchanging, such as parents divorcing, life coaching can help children to change their response to the situation. The situation may remain the same, but the method for managing it becomes more appropriate and resourceful, thus improving the child's social and emotional well-being and creating a more positive outlook and outcome.

Life coaching can help children and young people to:

- understand themselves better, including their triggers to negative emotion

- identify positive and negative influences

- build relationships with others

- manage difficult situation and emotions

- develop a positive, healthy self-image and identity

- manage anxiety and stress

- set and obtain goals

- improve self-esteem and self-confidence

- build resiliency and coping mechanisms.

Coaching is a particularly useful form of support for young people as it is action-oriented, practical, child-led and future-focused. Coaching tools and techniques lend themselves to one-to-one relationships, group work or whole-class work when used in a more general sense, offering a wide scope of applications. Life coaching can help to meet school well-being targets, develop a school or organization ethos of positivity and safety, contribute to students' academic skills and attainment, and improve school attendance. Coaching can also be used in informal settings, and can even be administered by children themselves.

When used in individual or group therapeutic settings, coaching can be a more practical form of support than traditional therapies, such as non-directive counselling. Some young people are unaccustomed to the counselling relationship, and find talking to an adult stranger about their problems to be unnatural and unnerving, given that their usual interaction with adults in formal settings is a relationship of adult instruction or power. In these settings children may be worried about 'getting it right' or fear being reprimanded for sharing their issues. Other forms of therapy are process-driven, such as art and play therapy that rely on the process of creating artwork or playing to be the language of therapeutic change. These creative therapies can be highly powerful and effective at facilitating emotional and behavioural change and working through complex problems and trauma, and are thus very appropriate for the needs of some children and young people. However, while effective, children may not have learned *how* to feel better and cope with their problems. The process may have worked to the extent that the children feel better equipped to function and feel positive about life, but are unable to concretely understand how this outcome was created, and therefore to replicate the success the next time their well-being is threatened. Added to this, creative therapy is unlikely to be offered to children with 'normal' problems, such as bullying, shyness or isolation at school, given the training and cost implications of providing a therapist. There are similar cost implications for school-based counselling that sometimes result in poorly trained and supervised staff being placed in the role of counsellor, or a member of school staff undertaking a dual role as teacher or teaching assistant and counsellor, muddying the waters of the counselling relationship for young people who may have concerns about confidentiality.

Life Coaching for Kids uses practical tools and techniques that, in simplified terms, could be used by young people between sessions, after coaching has come to an end, or by self-administering the tools without the need for a coach to be present. The practical activity and worksheet format of *Life Coaching for Kids* is designed specifically for children and young people who are typically adept and comfortable with this activity-based approach. Coaching also focuses on the future – setting goals and creating change – rather than looking back to the past, which some children have difficulty articulating, or which creates a negative cycle of focusing on the problem instead of the solution.

Coaching is a practical method to improve the well-being of young people and is applicable to a range of settings, including schools, youth and community settings, and in the home. With child and adolescent mental health problems seemingly on the rise, and youth well-being on the decline in many countries, there is a clear need to provide practical, targeted support to equip youth with the resources to better understand and help themselves, as well as provide educators, parents and youth workers with a toolkit of support to address issues as they occur.

Despite being from some of the wealthiest nations on the planet, children and young people living in countries such as the UK, USA and Canada are not thriving as well as their peers in other nations when it comes to well-being. The sheer breadth of issues faced by young people today from both deprived and affluent backgrounds speaks of the need to provide greater support to both parents and children to create a happy, prosperous, healthy and successful next generation. Life coaching tools and techniques can address many issues affecting youth well-being, in a practical, sustainable and cost-effective manner. Crucially, life coaching techniques seek to up-skill and educate young people to help themselves, building awareness for life.

Chapter summary

- Improving children's well-being is an effort of growing importance, at international, national and local levels.

- Affluent nations such as the UK and USA do not rate highly when it comes to child well-being.

- Addressing and improving youth well-being in schools is becoming more commonplace and expected.

- Life coaching can be a practical, cost-effective and multifaceted method of supporting general well-being and addressing specific issues affecting the physical and emotional health of youth.

Chapter 4

Life Coaching in Action

Life coaching is a multifaceted model of support, grounded in an empowering relationship between coach and client. It borrows tools, theories and concepts from a range of approaches, including psychotherapy, counselling, solution-focused brief therapy, CBT, motivational interviewing and creative approaches such as art and play therapy.

Coaching is, in essence, a style of communication – it is a positive exploration of a client's agenda, to empower and create change. The coaching relationship is central to the success of life coaching; rather than acting in the position of expert, a life coach assumes that clients are naturally resourceful and whole, have the capacity to improve their life situation, and can set and reach their goals and make life changes. In this way the coach is not trying to 'fix' clients, or mend something that is broken.

Central to the life coaching approach are underpinning beliefs on which the model is constructed. These beliefs create a mindset and an environment within which change can occur. Without these principles the foundation for the relationship and client's growth is weak, and a true coaching approach will not be achieved.

Life coaching beliefs

- The client is the expert.

- The client is unique, naturally resourceful and whole.

- Every situation has possibilities and problems have solutions.

- The client has the power of choice and can choose how to respond to life.

The life coach has an important role to play in the coaching relationship, but just as important is the client's role. The coach sets the tone and creates the environment within which change and growth can take place, and as such, the coach needs to be able to listen, communicate effectively, create a relationship of trust and respect and display empathy for the clients, so they feel comfortable enough to explore and share their life issues and challenge themselves to grow. Clients play an equal role – setting the agenda for coaching, committing to making behavioural change and undertaking tasks and exercises to allow those changes to take effect. The client's is not a passive role, waiting for the coach to impart wisdom, diagnose problems or analyse the client's past. Both coach and client are actively involved in this collaborative relationship.

The role of the coach

- To ensure the agenda for coaching is maintained.
- To help the client discover solutions, options and choices.
- To invite discovery and exploration by asking questions and prompting the client.
- To empower clients.
- To use their tools to teach and model skills to the client.
- To remain impartial, non-judgmental and empathetic to the client and the client's needs.
- To provide practical support where needed.
- To guide the client when needed.
- To be a 'cheerleader' for the client, identifying and acknowledging the client's resources, skills and expertise.

The concepts of life coaching

Life coaching is a form of support that is proactive and change-based. Coaching uses tools and concepts from a range of other therapeutic models with a teaching and/or modelling element. Coaches help clients to:

- identify areas of their life they need help with
- see issues from a different perspective
- choose their outcomes, responses and behaviours
- develop their life skills and resources to make those outcomes a reality.

Coaching helps clients to understand their life experiences and challenges from two perspectives:

- an external perspective: understanding the context in which their life is operating by exploring their behaviour and communication with others
- an internal perspective: exploring and addressing thoughts, feelings, values, beliefs and needs.

By exploring and understanding their external and internal perspective clients can build self-awareness, helping them to understand why they act in the way they do, which beliefs may be holding them back and how they can get better results. These are lifelong skills and perspectives that clients can maintain and build on in the future, so when a life issue arises post-coaching, clients have the necessary resources and tools to be able to help themselves.

Coaching provides clients with new behaviours and strategies for managing situations, in addition to building new ways to perceive situations. Coaching is built on the premise that we cannot change others, but we can change the way we relate to and react to others. Similarly, there may be life situations or events that are permanent and cannot be changed. Coaching can help people to positively deal with and manage their response to those situations, thus shifting their internal perspective and gaining a different, more positive outcome.

For example, a child may need coaching support to manage a difficult and conflicted family situation. Constant arguing at home is leaving the child feeling anxious and angry, as she struggles to understand why her parents are so controlling and inflexible. Power battles ensue, leaving both sides feeling wounded and disconnected. The child cannot change her living situation nor change her parents! This may result in her feeling disempowered, angry and out of control. Coaching can help the child to reframe her home situation, exploring her parents' perspective and building her communication skills and emotional literacy to better communicate her feelings to her parents. Coaching can also help her to find ways to experience more freedom and control in other parts of her life, while negotiating some middle ground with her parents.

Figure 4.1 highlights the main concepts of life coaching, including the role of the coach and some typical reasons why a person might access coaching.

Key Concepts of Life Coaching	Coaching Beliefs and Premise
• Solution focused and change-based • Person-centered • Practical and goal-oriented • Non-diagnosis based • Empowering – building clients' awareness and resources	• The client is the expert • The client is unique, naturally resourceful and whole • Every situation has possibilities and problems have solutions • The client has the power of choice and can choose how they respond to life
The Role of the Coach	**Why Clients Access Coaching**
• To ensure the agenda for coaching is maintained • Help the client discover solutions, options and choices • To empower their client • To play a teaching and modelling role and provide practical support where needed • To be a 'cheerleader' for the client, identifying and acknowledging their resources, skills and expertise	• To change a specific aspect of their life, e.g. lose weight, stop smoking, get a new job. • To change a general feeling or create a general sense of change, e.g. to feel more confident, to be happier, to feel more fulfilled • To learn practical skills and gain tools and strategies to use in specific or general life situations, e.g. relaxation skills, confidence building, public speaking, etc. • To gain therapeutic support, be listened to, and share their problems, while taking positive steps forward to a more successful, fulfilling future

Figure 4.1 : The Key Concepts of Life Coaching

Exploring similar models and approaches

Solution-focused brief therapy

Life coaching is similar in approach to a range of therapeutic models, and often borrows tools and strategies from these approaches. Solution-focused brief therapy (SFBT) is a similar model to life coaching, using a strengths-based approach to emphasize the resources that people possess and how these can be applied to a positive change process. Like coaching, and unlike traditional counselling and psychotherapy, SFBT focuses on strengths and creating a life without the problem, rather than a detailed analysis of the problem (Gingerich and Eisengart 2000). SFBT yields rapid, enduring change, and a high degree of client satisfaction (Stalker, Levene and Coady 1999). SFBT is now used in a variety of settings including schools, mental health settings, prisons, addiction treatment centres and hospitals in both the UK and USA (Miller, Hubble and Duncan 1996).

Like life coaching, SFBT encourages clients to consider how they would like things to change and to explore how that might happen. This assumes that clients want to change and have the capacity to envision and make those changes happen. Research conducted by the University of York in the UK found that SFBT showed promise in working with students in schools, particularly with those deemed 'at-risk' and needing support to manage behaviour and conduct problems (Kim and Franklin 2009).

Cognitive behavioural therapy

Cognitive behavioural therapy (CBT) originated from the work of American psychiatrist Dr Aaron T. Beck. CBT is a form of behavioural therapy, helping people to change their behaviour to gain better outcomes in life. The overarching principle of CBT is that a person's thoughts and feelings influence their behaviour. By becoming more aware of conscious and unconscious (or automatic) thoughts, a person can identify how those thoughts affect their mood, emotional state and actions. A CBT client will identify unresourceful thinking patterns and explore their core beliefs that might create those unhelpful thoughts.

For example, a child keeps experiencing bullying, despite moving to a number of different schools. On exploration, the child notices that her thoughts about other children and school are pervasively negative. She expects to be bullied, thinking that every other student is 'out to get her' and that school is not a safe place. These thoughts and beliefs leave the child guarded and wary, perhaps appearing unconfident and isolating herself from others. Others may perceive the child as a natural target for bullying.

By learning to identify and replace negative and unresourceful thoughts with more realistic, positive alternatives, the child can develop positive feelings about her experience and a stronger emotional state, and therefore create positive outcomes and behaviours. In this way CBT clients will learn more effective ways of coping with their problems, and more effective problem-solving skills.

CBT theories and strategies are often used in life coaching to build clients' awareness and help them to move forward, and the practical approach is particularly useful for working with children and young people. CBT has been found to be effective for a range of issues, including depression (Watanabe *et al.* 2007), traumatic stress (Stallard *et al.* 2007) and obsessive compulsive disorder (OCD) (O'Kearney *et al.* 2010).

Neuro-linguistic programming

Neuro-linguistic programming (NLP) was developed in the mid-1970s by John Grinder and Richard Bandler in the USA, by gathering examples of excellence to allow people to reproduce the approaches, mindset and methods used by those experts. NLP explores a person as a whole mind-body system, where mind and body are connected. NLP theorizes that there is a connection between the neurological processes of the brain ('neuro'), the language a person uses ('linguistic') and behavioural patterns learned through experience ('programming'). NLP attests that these processes, language and behavioural patterns can be re-programmed and changed to create a better life experience or to achieve a specific goal. NLP emphasizes learning as the key to personal change and development. Dilts, for example, states that a person has 'systematic, patterned connections between neurological processes ("neuro"), language ("linguistic") and learned behavioural strategies ("programming")' (Dilts 1980, p.2).

NLP is a technique used in a variety of contexts and within a range of therapeutic approaches. NLP techniques are found in hypnotherapy, coaching and psychotherapy. NLP in coaching is explored further in Chapter 11.

Counselling versus coaching

While the basis of life coaching and person-centred counselling may be similar, there are marked differences, and life coaches or people using coaching tools should not consider themselves professional counsellors, who would have a different role and method of supporting clients. Person-centred or humanistic counselling aims to support the growth of the whole person, as does life coaching, but differs in terms of being a largely non-directive form of support, where clients will lead the session and set their own agenda. Person-centred counsellors believe in the client's propensity toward growth and 'self-actualization', and aim to create an appropriate atmosphere for growth to take place, including through the creation of a relationship of depth between client and counsellor. Life coaching also supports the 'self-actualization' of a client towards positive growth and development, and the teaching or modelling of the skills necessary to do so. Self-actualization is the process of realizing one's own potential.

Person-centred counsellors do not have an agenda or work plan, and will view themselves as sitting alongside clients, being witnesses to their lives and letting clients tell their story and history. There is typically little focus on working proactively to avoid future problems, modelling skills, attitudes or behaviours or setting goals to support clients to make changes, which is the focus of life coaching. In contrast, life coaches will utilize the specific theories and attitudes of counsellors, but will additionally employ more directive techniques and strategies to support clients to make changes. Life coaches may provide therapeutic support, but are also teachers and guides for clients to make positive changes, at times taking the role of mentor, at other times leader (such as modelling a skill or behaviour for clients to adapt as their own), or embodying the role of the traditional idea of a 'coach' – being the client's advocate, building the client's confidence, providing encouragement, communicating a belief in the client's abilities, and so on.

One of the main aspects of life coaching that differentiates it from humanistic counselling or other forms of therapy is the *practical* support provided by the coach to empower clients to find their own way forward. With the skills clients have learned or the knowledge they have gained from working in cooperation with their coach, they are empowered and equipped to move forward, no longer needing the support of the coach, and being able to apply the same techniques and perspective to future problems. While many people can feel as though they can make positive changes with the help or advice of someone close to them, when a similar problem arises or they experience difficulties in another area of their life, they may not have learned how to navigate their way through the issue. Therefore they return to the feelings of 'stuckness' or disempowerment, having not learned how to cope. For example, clients who learn in coaching how to present themselves more confidently and make small talk with strangers to improve their social life and meet new friends may also find their new skills of use when attending a job interview. Clients have also learned how to find support when needed in future situations, ensuring they are not reliant on the support of the coach, therapist or another professional, but are truly in control of their own growth and well-being.

A counsellor, psychotherapist or psychiatrist would likely build a long-lasting relationship with a client, aiming to help clients over a number of sessions. In life coaching, sessions can be brief, with some coaches and clients meeting three to six times to explore a specific theme or issue. However, counselling or other forms of therapy might be utilized in conjunction with coaching. Counselling might assist clients to explore underlying issues and deep-seated emotional trauma, while coaching or other forms of brief intervention might help clients to address practical problems or create a shift in the here-and-now. Alternatively, clients may only be ready to work on explicit issues or goals and feel ready for therapy.

For example, a client may present for coaching with a need to gain more confidence to be able to meet a romantic partner. Through exploration with the client it becomes apparent that her low confidence in this area might be in part due to witnessing domestic abuse in the childhood home, or an abuse of trust by a previous partner. The client may not be willing or able to see the link between past and present events and feelings, which may even have been suppressed. But over time the client might feel sufficiently supported to be able to access longer-term therapy to explore or deal with her past.

Figure 4.2 provides examples of potential coaching clients, and counselling clients, to help differentiate between the two.

Potential Life Coaching Client	Potential Counselling Client
A middle aged woman wants to quit her current job to start her own business. She needs help with practical skills and action planning, and building the confidence to take the leap.	A middle aged woman wants to quit her current job to start her own business. She is facing considerable resistance from her family resulting in conflict at home. She feels lost and confused. Her anxiety about doing the right thing by her family or following her dreams has resulted in anxiety and depression.
A teenage girl is experiencing bullying at school and she is struggling to make friends. She wants help to build her confidence and social skills to be able to approach people and manage unwanted attention. She is looking for practical advice about where to meet people and how to deflect bullying taunts.	A teenage girl has experienced persistent, pervasive bullying since childhood. The bullying has followed her from school to school and considerably impacted upon her psyche. She has internalized the messages received by her tormentors and believes herself to be ugly, fat, stupid and so on. She has recently started self harming and trying drastic measures to lose weight.
A young boy has been having difficulties sleeping since moving into a new family home. He is restless and anxious at bedtime, and increasingly this anxiety is building throughout the day. He finds it difficult to relax and needs help to build practical relaxation skills and methods to reduce his anxiety, reframing his perception of sleep.	A young boy has been having difficulties sleeping and is displaying anxiety and behavioural problems in school. Child protection concerns have been raised about his home situation and it has come to light that his father is physically and emotionally abusive to his mother and elder siblings.

Figure 4.2: Potential Coaching and Counselling Clients

When working with children and young people it is important to be aware of potential child protection issues or indicators that specialist therapeutic support might be needed. If a child presents deeper psychological issues or a need for more intensive therapy it would also be important to work within the coach's level of proficiency, being aware of the child's needs and best interests as central to the work.

Young people surveyed by the British Association for Counselling and Psychotherapy, on behalf of the Welsh Government for a report into counselling in schools shared that they wanted a counsellor to have proper training and to be experienced. The counsellor should be an understanding person who should talk and not just listen. Some students felt they wanted the counsellor to give advice (BACP 2007). One young person stated how important a listening ear was for youth:

> The teenage years are a time of great change...some of the things going on in pupils' heads [are hard to] fully understand. Talking to someone confidentially about what they are thinking may help them sort out the meaning of what they are thinking, like with cases of bullying and self-confidence issues, counseling would be a help. (BACP 2007, p.43)

There are both marked differences between traditional counselling and life coaching, and similarities in approach, as highlighted in Figure 4.3. A qualified counsellor, psychologist or psychotherapist will likely undergo years of training at varying levels and commit to continued professional development, a code of practice and ethical guidelines. This is usually not the case for life coaches – training is quicker, cheaper and far less intense, often not requiring trainees to undergo any practical casework. This is appropriate at the level of training, so long as trainee coaches don't presume to have become experts or therapists adept at working beyond their level of competency. Such people could potentially do damage to clients by presuming to 'diagnose' mental health concerns, labelling clients with a disorder they likely do not have, or by encouraging clients to explore deep-seated issues that they are not ready (or willing) to do at that time, and perhaps weren't even aware of.

Clients may have specifically chosen to access coaching to help with surface issues because they didn't feel ready or able to access therapy – coaches presuming themselves as expert therapists may force clients to do so, damaging the client–coach relationship, potentially causing emotional distress to clients, and even deterring clients from seeking help elsewhere in the future. Some clients may – by the nature of seeking help – be in a fragile and susceptible emotional state that could easily be exasperated by a coach acting in such a manner.

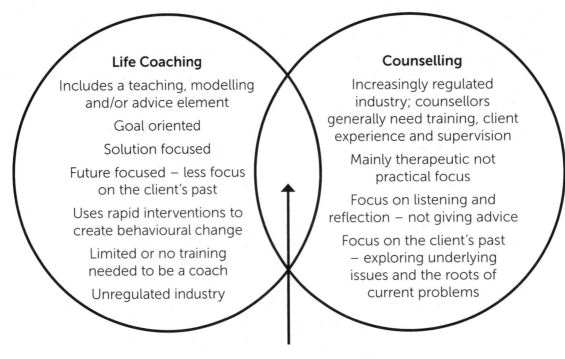

Life Coaching

Includes a teaching, modelling and/or advice element

Goal oriented

Solution focused

Future focused – less focus on the client's past

Uses rapid interventions to create behavioural change

Limited or no training needed to be a coach

Unregulated industry

Counselling

Increasingly regulated industry; counsellors generally need training, client experience and supervision

Mainly therapeutic not practical focus

Focus on listening and reflection – not giving advice

Focus on the client's past – exploring underlying issues and the roots of current problems

Both Coaching and Counselling

Are not a quick fix or magic wand

Are person-centred; putting the client at the centre of the relationship and working to their agenda

Aim to help the client self-actualize, positively grow

Figure 4.3: Life Coaching and Counselling: Similarities and Differences

A life coaching case study

A young woman, Sally, is accessing one-to-one life coaching to help with her lack of confidence. Sally is able to generally articulate her lack of confidence but is unable to specifically state how she would like her life to be different or the changes she wishes to make.

Session 1

Within the first session Sally explores what being confident means to her, and identifies when she lacks confidence. She begins to realize that her lack of confidence is not a universal problem – she is confident in situations when she feels comfortable and at ease, and with people she trusts, such as her family. Using a scaling tool, Sally identifies the parts of her life that are affected by low confidence, and how her low confidence manifests itself, such as when she is in big groups of students at school, particularly girls, and when she is in class. Sally and her coach explore how she might look, feel and act if she were confident, and identify a person that embodies that sense of confidence that Sally feels eludes her. They explore the characteristics of that person, and her coach models some aspects of confident body language for Sally to try and practise at home. Sally identifies a few additional ways she can practise being confident, and they agree this as her homework before the next session, such as putting her hand up in class once or twice to answer a question, and looking people in the eye when she is talking to them.

TOOLS AND TECHNIQUES USED

- Identifying the problem; Goal setting; Scaling; Modelling; Skills practice.

Session 2

Within the second session Sally and her coach review the homework and progress journal she has been keeping. They explore how it felt and the impact of trying the confidence activities. Sally shared how easy the small confidence steps were, and they set goals to try somewhat bigger steps next time, such as making conversation with an acquaintance or stranger. With the help of her coach, Sally identifies her thoughts, feelings and behaviours when she is in a situation where she doesn't feel confident. Sally and her coach explore some 'automatic thoughts', such as 'I am not good enough' and 'They won't like me', and identify the impact of these thoughts on her behaviour and therefore on her interactions with others. Sally and her coach explore the validity of these thoughts and try some reframing techniques to create a more resourceful mindset.

TOOLS AND TECHNIQUES USED

- Feedback; CBT – thoughts, feelings, behaviour loop; Exploring automatic thoughts; Reframing.

Session 3

In the final session, Sally and her coach review her progress and the results of her homework. They explore where progress has been made using the original scaling tool used in the first session, and explore where further progress may need to be centred. Sally reports that she feels more confident interacting with strangers, but is still not confident around girls in her peer group. Sally and her coach explore some of her automatic thoughts relating to her peer group, and her coach takes Sally through a simple visualization, imagining her to be with her peers looking relaxed, confident and happy, and interacting with the other girls effortlessly. Sally confirms she will continue using the visualization in her own time. Her coach uses an anchoring technique to secure the feelings of confidence within Sally's mind, so that she might draw on those feelings when needed. Sally's coach challenges her to think about what might be the worst thing that could happen if she were to act confidently with her peers and try out the skills she has learned, to test the validity of her negative thoughts. Sally works through the possible outcomes and she and her coach score each one on the likelihood that it might happen. Sally realizes that it is unlikely that she might be laughed at or bullied for smiling at another student or making conversation in the lunchroom, for example.

Finally, Sally and her coach explore what happens for her physically when she feels lacking in confidence, and Sally identifies that she starts to feel quite anxious, nervous, sweaty and on edge, which exacerbates her negative thinking. Her coach models some simple relaxation and stress management techniques she can use when not feeling confident to bring her back to her natural state. Again, Sally can practise and use these techniques in her own time. Sally and her coach review her progress and set goals for her post-coaching. They list her newly developed skills and resources, and make an action plan for the future, writing ideas for how Sally can cope if she feels unconfident in future scenarios.

TOOLS AND TECHNIQUES USED

- Feedback; Goal setting; Scaling; CBT; Visualization; Anchoring; Reframing; Exploring mind–body connection; Relaxation techniques; Action planning.

These tools and techniques are discussed in more detail in Part 2.

Chapter summary

- Life coaching believes every person to be the expert on him or herself, with the necessary resources to solve his or her own problems. Every problem has a solution.

- Life coaching is a positive, change-based form of support that helps people to identify and see issues from a different perspective and change their behaviours for a better result.

- Life coaching is not counselling or other forms of therapy, although it might borrow perspectives, tools and strategies from other theories and approaches.

Chapter 5

Using Life Coaching for Kids in Schools

The concept of educating the whole child has become of pressing importance for schools around the world in recent years. With poor marks for child well-being levels in many affluent and supposedly well-resourced countries such as the UK and USA, schools have been increasingly tasked with developing children's social and emotional skills, and physical and mental health, as government and local policy makers note that academic success alone does not necessarily translate into good well-being.

For some children the environmental, social and health factors impacting on their well-being naturally translate into low school attainment and engagement. Without school-based efforts to monitor and support as well as educate these children, they might fall through the gaps of society, becoming yet another statistic.

Some argue that the traditional role of teacher is becoming increasingly blurred, with added responsibilities and tasks turning a classroom teacher into counsellor, family therapist, social worker or parent. As any hard-working, caring teachers will attest, it is difficult to draw the line when needy children come to their attention, and there is certainly a duty of care and level of responsibility towards the children and young people the schools serve.

Regardless of the politics of the teaching role, it is evident that school-based well-being programmes are on the increase, both mandated by local or national policy, and voluntarily introduced by schools to meet the needs of staff and students. Many schools report that positive behaviour management strategies, Social and Emotional Learning (SEL) programmes, respect and empathy programmes, anti-bullying schemes, school counselling services and a host of other approaches all form pieces of the education puzzle, helping to grow and educate students ready for life beyond the classroom. Purely focusing on academic attainment and results can fail to ensure young people are equipped with the skills necessary for life. Well-being and SEL programmes build students' critical thinking skills, empathy, social and relationship skills, resilience and motivation to succeed – all pieces of the success puzzle.

Life coaching compliments SEL programmes and other efforts to improve children and young people's health, and can help schools to meet their well-being targets for students. Coaching can be utilized in schools in a variety of ways, including:

- whole school

- curriculum-based

- pastoral support.

The nature of the coaching model lends itself to a variety of applications and can be used in both primary and secondary school settings.

Coaching as a whole-school approach

The most fundamental and powerful implementation of life coaching in a school setting is the creation of a whole-school holistic model, where all staff members have a working understanding of the coaching model and tools to use in teaching, learning, staff training and development, behaviour management, assessment and other daily aspects of school life. Embedding life coaching as a holistic model and ethos of support across the school can assist with:

- positive behaviour management

- improving attainment and attendance, including learners' engagement with school

- promoting respectful relationships across the school, between staff and students

- developing students' self-management, guidance and regulation skills

- supporting students to reach self-defined academic and non-academic goals

- creating a whole-school ethos of support, collaboration, problem-solving and empowerment

- promoting students' autonomy, independence and aspirations

- developing positive relationships with parents and guardians, including providing tools to help parents support their child's development and education

- providing tools to assist with staff development, supervision and peer learning for teachers

- measuring and promoting well-being, and assisting individual children with their social and emotional needs, physical and mental health.

Training all members of staff in the life coaching approach and coaching skills is a significant and innovative undertaking that will not be suited to all schools. A whole-school approach would require a financial and time commitment and a potentially staged approach, depending on the size of the school. A whole-school model would ideally be led from the top down, where the initiative is supported and mandated by senior management, as opposed to the passionate idea of a few lone members of staff – although the buy-in of those 'on the ground' is also crucial.

Any whole-school approach must be consistent and coordinated, with all members of the school community working towards a shared mission and using a shared approach. Empowering students to set their own goals or use problem-solving skills to resolve conflict in one classroom will have limited reach if the next class or year group uses the opposite approach.

Coaching as a whole-school approach might include working with students to set classroom and school rules for behaviour; encouraging students to set weekly or monthly goals linked to academic and non-academic attainment and levels; self-reflection exercises to build social and emotional literacy; developing students' basic coaching skills to resolve peer conflicts and friendship issues; and creating a framework for staff coaching, modelling and peer support. There are many other applications for life coaching in a whole-school setting that can be developed and enhanced over time.

Good teachers are natural coaches – they identify children's strengths and help overcome their weaknesses. They motivate and encourage, providing constructive feedback and building children's skills to make progress towards their goals. They model important processes, including interpersonal skills and emotional literacy, and are focused on solutions, not problems. However, coaching as an educative approach may be a foreign or completely alien concept for some members of the school community, and therefore difficult to embrace. Those more accustomed to a traditional and authoritarian model of schooling may be less comfortable with the life coaching concept and approach, such as teaching and learning led solely by adults, punitive measures to manage student behaviour, or a focus on academic attainment over and above social and emotional development. For those schools not ready or unable to fully embed coaching as a whole-school approach, the life coaching model might be better suited to assisting individual students with well-being needs, or as a useful addition to the curriculum.

Life coaching in the curriculum

Increasingly, schools are being tasked with providing education that develops the citizenship, health and personal and social skills of students, alongside the core and traditional subjects. In the UK many schools deliver PSHE lessons within the National Curriculum, while elsewhere these themes are embedded within traditional subjects, such as exploring the effects of substance abuse through English literature, or interpersonal and relationship skills in history lessons.

As the improvement of youth well-being becomes a pressing issue for schools, the curriculum is adapting to encompass measures to develop healthy, confident, resilient and socially competent students. The *Life Coaching for Kids* tools and techniques can be integrated into existing schemes of work to benefit all students, not just those children with an identified need. The coaching process and activities can build young people's confidence and self-esteem; assist with setting and reaching academic goals; help young people to explore the impact of risky behaviours; build self-awareness and self-regulation; strengthen coping skills; prevent bullying; and improve students' relationships.

Coaching as pastoral support

In the UK 1.6 million children have SEN, such as dyslexia, autism, attention deficit hyperactivity disorder (ADHD), or emotional and behavioural difficulties (DfE 2012), while many more suffer from physical, social and emotional problems that impact on their attainment, school attendance and quality of life. Nine per cent of all children aged 5–17 in the USA have been diagnosed with ADHD, which can manifest as an inability to control behaviour and pay attention, an increase from 7 per cent since 2000 (Akinbami *et al.* 2011).

Pastoral support is a crucial element of school life, given the potential impact of life problems on children's ability to learn. A friendship fallout, however trivial it may seem to adults, can totally occupy a child's mind, leaving the child anxious and unwilling to attend school. Bullying can create fear and trauma for the young person who is waiting to be attacked at any moment, while a serious eating disorder might leave a young person physically and emotionally incapacitated to learn. For other children, low academic ability or behavioural problems can result in a lack of confidence and self-belief, or cast them apart from other students.

Twenty-first century living, despite all its trappings, is rapidly making childhood and adolescence a time fraught with challenges: the 'must-have' fashion accessories that, if not owned, can leave you susceptible to bullying; the 24/7 nature and permanence of online communication; the near constant influence of media ideals and messages for how we should look and act – the pressure on young people today is immense, and can naturally translate into low confidence, self-esteem, risky behaviours and poor choices.

A survey by the Office for National Statistics in the UK on child and adolescent mental health found that 11.5 per cent (or about 510,000) of UK young people aged between 11 and 16 have a mental disorder (Green *et al.* 2005). In the USA suicide is the third leading cause of death for young people between the ages of 10 and 24, resulting in 4600 lives lost each year (CDC 2012). Regardless of the issue, intervention is important when young people are prevented from fully participating in school life, being fulfilled and ready to learn. Intervention is critical when a young person's health is in jeopardy.

The generally agreed measures for children and young people's well-being include material/economic well-being; good health and safety; educational attainment; managing behaviours and risk; good housing and living environment; and a positive family and social environment. Schools are well placed to improve students' well-being through a variety of informal and formal support mechanisms, including:

- addressing personal and social issues within the school curriculum

- providing student counselling

- offering opportunities for young people's growth and development such as volunteering or a school leadership role

- healthy school initiatives including promoting physical activity

- classroom-based positive behaviour and social-emotional programmes

- targeted support for vulnerable students including referrals to external agencies and support for children and families in need.

Life coaching can complement this array of pastoral and support services for identified students in need. Coaching can be offered as an addition to school-based counselling or therapy, as a standalone service, or an informal or sporadic form of group support.

Working on a one-to-one basis with a child or in a group setting, coaching provides a framework and toolkit to address specific issues (such as bullying) or improve general well-being (such as improving confidence and self-esteem). Coaching is practical, fun, engaging and not overly time intensive – individual life coaching is usually offered over three to six sessions of approximately one hour per session, although this is dependent on the age and ability level of the child and their presenting issues. For example, a young student, a child with significant SEN or low cognition and understanding, or a child with complex issues and needs might require shorter sessions over a longer period of time.

Setting the scene for school-based coaching

Using the *Life Coaching for Kids* tools and activities in a school-based or other formal setting (such as within a youth centre or family support service) can be a practical and productive way to support the needs of children and young people, particularly those aged 10–16. Before providing one-to-one or group coaching support, practitioners may wish to reflect on the following practical considerations.

Setting the tone for coaching

Coaching, like all forms of pastoral or therapeutic support, should not be a punitive measure, invoked as a response to poor behaviour or rule-breaking. The very nature of coaching is collaborative, child-centred, solution-focused and empowering. Coaching places the focus and goals (and therefore control) of the sessions into the hands of the child, with the coach acting as guide and supporter. If life coaching is to be an effective source of support for children, this concept must be understood and communicated across the school, and modelled by those providing coaching.

Creating the right environment

Consider where life coaching sessions (either individual or group) will take place. A dedicated room or space away from usual footfall with some degree of privacy is best, where children can speak openly about their issues, thoughts and feelings without fear of being overheard or ridiculed. A comfortable environment is also key – conducting sessions in a teacher's lounge, staff room or a staff member's office may be frightening and unfamiliar territory for a child. A space with comfortable chairs and a table to work at is best, with access to resources if needed, such as paper, marker pens and crayons. Group sessions should be centred round one table if possible, with each person sitting on a chair of the same height. The coach or facilitator should work to create an atmosphere where each person feels of equal value – therefore the adult should be seated with the children, not stood up in front of them, and should sit in a chair of similar height and size to the children's, for example. In this way coaches communicate that they are part of the session, and not leaders in charge.

Choosing the right person to coach

In schools or settings where a teaching or non-teaching staff member will provide coaching sessions (as opposed to an external professional or counsellor) it is important to ensure the right person is chosen for the role. A coach requires excellent interpersonal skills, the ability to listen and communicate with children openly and honestly and an understanding of their needs. They must understand the role of a coach and should ideally embody the principles of coaching, demonstrating a belief in the ability of young people to resolve their own problems and the importance of empowering youth. Those delivering life coaching must be able to differentiate between their position as coach and their other roles within the school – coaching is not punitive, and although it might contain a teaching, modelling or advice-giving element, it is not a teaching process. Schools should consider carefully who provides one-to-one or group coaching. Some young people may struggle to understand the concept of the process if a classroom teacher is also providing one-to-one or group coaching: the child may mistakenly believe coaching to be a punishment for academic failure or poor behaviour, or a homework or study skills programme. Setting clear expectations at the outset of coaching with both students and parents can help to alleviate any confusion.

Knowing the limitations of coaching

Coaching can be a highly effective model of support for children and young people of varying ages and with varying needs. However, it is not a magic wand or 'cure all', and will not be a suitable response for every child. Coaching might:

- uncover deeper or underlying concerns that necessitate a referral for specialist support, for example, self-harm, an eating disorder, substance misuse, or abuse

- help with surface issues, while a child gains formal therapeutic or issue-specific support for underlying or psychological concerns, for example, coaching will work on friendship issues and relationship skills while a child receives psychotherapy for mental health problems

- not be right for the child – he may not like the format of coaching, feel unable to engage in a group coaching scenario or be unwilling and unmotivated to set goals or explore his presenting issues at that time. A child should never be forced to undertake coaching – this contravenes the model of child-centred and child-led support.

Other factors to consider

Before implementing one-to-one or group coaching sessions, you should also consider the following points:

- how you will inform and communicate with parents, if necessary

- the level of confidentiality in coaching sessions and how this will be communicated to children and parents

- which students will be offered coaching and how it will be explained to them

- how you will promote life coaching if it is to be a self-referral form of support for children and young people

- how you will measure a student's progress through coaching to demonstrate success of the model

- whether coaches will work with young people for a set number of sessions or on an open-ended basis

- whether a generic coaching service will be offered to respond to any youth problem, or if coaching will be issue-specific, for example, just to support young people affected by bullying

- records you will keep, such as attendance records by name, numbers of young people accessing a coaching service, types of presenting issues, duration of sessions, students and parents' feedback about coaching (this might help to fund a larger service in the future).

Confidentiality is an important issue to consider if establishing a formal one-to-one or group coaching service in a school or youth setting. Counselling is typically regarded as confidential unless clients indicate (or a counsellor is significantly concerned) that they might cause harm to themselves or others, in which case the counsellor has a duty of care and responsibility to break client–counsellor confidentiality. This may involve discussing the issue of concern with a supervisor, making a referral for further support or contacting emergency services or the police in extreme cases.

When coaching children and young people consider how much information may need to be shared with teachers, support staff or parents, or whether this would harm the coaching relationship. For example, a coach may wish to share the session themes and the child's concerns with his parents after coaching so the child can be supported between sessions. Be mindful that the child or young person will need to know the degree of confidentiality that will be maintained in coaching, as this might affect the information he feels willing to share. Coaches may wish to instead maintain confidentiality as in traditional counselling settings, and work to encourage and empower the young person to share information with his parents or guardians himself. Always reiterate the confidentiality agreement to children attending coaching sessions so they are perfectly clear what information may be shared, with whom and when.

Informal or group coaching is less likely to be as strictly confidential, but all participants should be made aware of the importance of keeping what is said private within the space and to avoid gossiping. This is particularly important when working the groups of children. Coaches may wish to create a group contract or list of promises for behaviour for each member of the group to sign in the first coaching session, to refer back to when needed.

Maintaining confidentiality and discretion is also important for adults – coaches should avoid gossiping about children's problems or issues brought to coaching even if no specific confidentiality clause has been set. This is unethical and unprofessional.

Life coaching has numerous applications in schools and other formal settings, and finding the right approach is important. Coaching might be an addition to a practitioner's toolkit, as he uses the tools and ideas in an informal way to enhance teaching, learning and relationships with students. This practitioner might use goal-setting activities with students at the beginning of each academic year or school term, or utilize a coaching perspective in his teaching. For others, life coaching techniques will be better suited to working with a whole class as a part of the school's SEL programme, such as a weekly coaching session to build confidence, self-esteem, relationship skills, critical thinking skills and self-management. A more formal approach of semi-therapeutic one-to-one or group coaching might be the best fit for identified children, to meet the needs of students and the school.

Chapter summary

- Life coaching can complement school-based programmes and support to improve youth well-being.

- Coaching can be used as a whole-school approach, within the curriculum or as part of pastoral support on a one-to-one or group basis for children with an identified need.

- Schools need to consider how they will implement life coaching, and the various practical issues to take into account before a service or programme is initiated.

Chapter 6

Life Coaching for Kids at Home

As many parents will attest, raising children in the 21st century is no easy job. The stresses of modern-day living, constant communication, media overload and hectic schedules can fragment families and place a strain on children's physical and emotional health. The days of sitting down to dinner each night to connect as a family are sadly long gone for many, with both parents having to work full time, single-parent households relying on childcare support, and the lure of laptops, TVs and games consoles in children's bedrooms making family time rare.

Roughly 60 per cent of two-parent households in the USA with children under the age of 18 have two working parents (Mattingly and Bianchi 2003), which, although an often necessary requirement to make ends meet, can cause family discord. A report by the Pew Research Center in Washington DC (2013) found that many parents find it difficult to balance home and work responsibilities. Fifty-three per cent of all working parents with children under the age of 18 say it is difficult for them to balance the responsibilities of their job with the responsibilities of their family, with both parents reporting feeling stressed about juggling work and family life.

The Pew study also found that 40 per cent of working mothers and 34 per cent of working fathers said they always felt rushed, with a third of parents worrying about whether they spent enough time with their children. Similar findings are echoed in Australia, with around 40 per cent of women and 30 per cent of men reporting being often or always rushed or pressed for time (Cassells, Gong and Duncan 2011).

Spending quality time as a family can be the casualty of rising living costs and a need for both parents to work. An assessment of the UK's progress to becoming a family-friendly society was produced by the Family and Parenting Institute (FPI) (2012), and found that high childcare costs, high costs of living and the subsequent rise in weekly hours that couples with children need to work all contribute to a poor quality of life for too many families. The Family Report Card uses a school-style grade and found that the UK has a long way to go, with a score of just D+.

A similar picture is evident in the USA. Research conducted by the University of Southern California Annenberg Center for the Digital Future (2013) found that 48 per cent of internet users said they were sometimes or often ignored because another member of the household spent too much time online, while 92 per cent said they were ignored because a household member spent too much time on a mobile device – either talking, texting or web browsing.

The challenges for families of all shapes and sizes only appear to be growing, and with the added financial and time pressures placed on parents and carers, it is easy for children's needs to go unnoticed. Despite knowing more about the importance of maintaining young people's emotional well-being and health than ever before, mental health problems, including severe illnesses such as acute depression and anxiety, are only growing in prevalence for young people.

The impact of significant problems at home is well researched and clear. Parental separation and divorce, the illness of a parent or caregiver, domestic abuse and young people providing the role of primary caregiver for their parent or guardian are just a few examples of complex issues affecting children's physical and emotional health, happiness, academic attainment and school attendance. Children witnessing domestic abuse, for example, are at an increased risk of becoming victims of abuse themselves (UNICEF 2006), are more likely to experience personality and behavioural problems such as psychosomatic illnesses, depression, suicidal tendencies and bed-wetting (Kernic *et al.* 2003), and are at a greater risk of substance misuse, juvenile pregnancy and criminal behaviour than those raised in homes without violence (Herrera and McCloskey 2001).

Major life events and problems at home can have a devastating impact on children's current and future well-being, but are not the only causes for concern. A lack of family time and stressed-filled parenting can have an altogether more subtle impact on child well-being. Busy parents may be less likely to notice their child falling behind at school, or withdrawing because of bullying, for example. Children may have fewer opportunities to communicate with their parents about important issues, or to share worries, fear and upset, which can result in young people internalizing their problems, withdrawing or developing low self-esteem.

While some problems at home start to affect young people at school, such as parental divorce or domestic abuse, similarly, problems at school can pervade the safety and sanctuary of home. Thanks in part to ubiquitous contact, social networking and always-connected mobile technology, children's problems at school become problems at home, inescapable and often omnipresent. The bullying taunts of the playground follow a child home as harassing text messages or threatening Facebook posts. Friendship problems in the classroom become marked by silence on social networking sites at home.

Without opportunities to share, discuss and gain reassurance from parents, children can become locked in their problems and fail to learn the coping strategies and processes to resolve issues that build resilience and are essential for later life.

Carving out time to be together, talk and share as a family or one-on-one between parent and child is no easy feat. Family time is often centred round activities, such as watching TV, playing games or leisure activities outside the home, which, although important and fun, aren't always opportunities to connect and talk about problems or concerns, or to share victories and accomplishments. Making special time can help children and parents to feel more connected, offer opportunities to listen and learn from one another, and build essential problem-solving skills, emotional literacy, resilience and motivation.

The life coaching approach and tools can help families to work on problems together, set and reach shared goals, or support individual children with their needs. The coaching model is similar to the role of a parent: coaching relationships are built on trust, mutual respect, openness, support and empathy. A coach's mission is to support clients in the successful reach of their goals, bearing witness to their personal development and growth as they create life-affirming changes. A parent's mission is similar – to see their child grow and develop, personally, socially, academically and emotionally, and for children to realize their potential while living a happy and fulfilled life.

No parent could want less for their children than to be happy and healthy and to feel rewarded in their pursuits, career and home life. The parallels between coach and parent are numerous: coaches support, challenge, educate, motivate, encourage and hopefully bear witness to their client's personal growth, just as most parents strive to do. Parents will often act in the role of coach to their children, helping guide them through difficult situations and periods, to reach goals, whether small or large.

Taking the next step by using the coaching tools can help parents to support their children through challenging periods or problems, such as friendship fallout, or the difficult transition from child to adolescent, where hormones and body changes can wreak havoc emotionally. Using coaching tools in the home can build happy, confident and self-aware children, while parents feel more aware of their child's needs and better equipped to tackle problems and raise well-balanced, optimistic children.

Coaching your child

When school or friendship problems rear their heads it can be difficult for parents to know the best way to support their child. Do you approach the parents of your child's best friend when they've had a falling out? Will reporting bullying to the school make matters worse? Is tutoring the answer when your child is falling behind or disengaging from school? For many families doing the right thing can feel like a minefield, particularly when the need to encourage children to find solutions to their own problems is also paramount. Coming to the rescue each time a child is in need of help is a natural step for any caring adult, but giving children the tools and awareness to resolve their own problems – with our help – will build crucial lifelong competencies.

The *Life Coaching for Kids* approach and tools are well suited to an informal, encouraging relationship of support between parent or carer, and child. Coaching tools can be used when an issue needs discussion and resolution, or on a regular basis to keep children focused, confident, self-aware and feeling positive. As in formal settings, such as at school, or when used in a more formal and structured approach, such as an anti-bullying group for children at risk of becoming victimized, coaching should always be a voluntary and child-led approach. When coaching tools are used at home they should be viewed as a fun, shared process of exploration and learning, rather than a punishment for poor behaviour, or a continuation of homework and school tasks.

Using coaching in a one-on-one format between parent or carer and child will be a similar process to using coaching in a school or youth setting. Creating the right atmosphere and environment for coaching to take place is the first step to facilitating coaching, rather than a chat or discussion between parent and child. Finding a quiet space away from the rest of the family hustle and bustle is important, as is giving your undivided attention. Using life coaching with children can create a unique and uncommon space for children to feel heard, appreciated, understood and valued. Being fully present and connected with a child is so valuable in an age where we are often interrupted by the noise of the TV, by ringing phones and the impulse to immediately answer emails as they drop into our inbox.

The second step to setting the tone for a coaching relationship is to embody the role and attitude of a coach. Coaching in the home is obviously not a formal process – children should not feel as though they are being counselled or assessed by a professional, instead of spending quality and productive time with a parent or grandparent. However, to truly gain something from coaching and to enjoy the process, a child should be able to feel supported, listened to, respected and constructively challenged (where necessary). Therefore a parent or carer may need to put to one side their sometimes default responses of giving instruction or being in control that come with parenting territory.

Using life coaching with children is a trial and error approach. There is no 'one size fits all' answer to how to help and support children, and parents may find that the coaching tools are just as useful for them as they are for their child! Finding what works best may take time, and it may be the case that children will prefer to use the coaching techniques and resources alone at their own pace, or using them sporadically as a whole family works better for them.

Many of the tools and resources in Parts 2 and 3 of this book can be used by parents or carers in the home, to informally coach their children, but parents are encouraged to use their guidance when selecting the activities and approaches that best meet the needs of their child.

Tips for using coaching tools one-to-one

- *Make it fun:* coaching doesn't have to be a serious endeavour. Make a game out of the activities to help your child engage and enjoy using the tools.

- *Get involved:* try doing the activities too, to create a bond with your child and to help her view coaching as a positive process. For example, keep a journal alongside your child and compare notes, or spend ten minutes together each evening doing a relaxation exercise.

- *Be consistent:* if you and your child have decided on weekly special time together where you will use coaching tools and activities, try and keep that time sacred and regular.

- *Keep it short:* informal coaching doesn't need to be a rigid 30 minutes or hour session. Find what works for you and your child – perhaps use one of the activities for five minutes before bedtime, or spend ten minutes setting goals each week after completing homework.

- *Keep it positive:* be mindful of how you approach coaching with your child. Avoid labelling or making your child feel as though she has a problem. For example, if you are concerned about your child's lack of confidence, offer her coaching activities under the premise of fun games to make her feel happier, rather than activities to tackle her shyness problem.

- *Create a space for coaching:* create a space in or outside of the home where you and your child can be together without being interrupted. This time will be just as valued and important as the coaching process, and will help to build a strong relationship where your child feels listened to and supported.

Coaching for the whole family

In some households coaching can become part of the fabric of family life, helping all members of the family to reach their goals, feel listened to and heard, to understand and appreciate one another, find solutions to problems, and to stay connected.

Just as coaching tools can be used one-to-one between parent and child, so too can the whole family use many coaching activities and strategies informally. Time spent as a whole family unit is increasingly rare, and often centres on activities such as watching TV, going shopping, playing sports, or going to see a film – activities that don't necessarily encourage conversation and sharing. Creating a consistent opportunity for meeting as a family to talk about problems, share successes and set goals may be met with some resistance at first, particularly if mobile phones are not allowed and TVs are switched off! But persevering should pay off.

Simple coaching tools can be used to set family goals, deciding how each member of the family will contribute and share towards creating a happier home, or each individual can set their own goals for the week or month in a shared process. In this way all adults and children form part of the process, are accountable for the whole family's progress and happiness, and are aware of each other's needs. Parents setting goals alongside their offspring can help children to see them as real people with their own failings, challenges and dreams, while parents become more aware of what is going on in their children's lives and any issues they may have. Children can help parents to reach their goals, and vice versa, developing a more connected and cohesive household.

Using the tools to self-coach

Some children, particularly older adolescents, may prefer to use the coaching tools and activities unsupervised, guiding themselves through an individual process. Although not suited to all youngsters – particularly those who may need support to understand the activities, to identify issues they wish to explore, or to reflect on their progress – self-coaching is an important process that builds lifelong skills and competencies. In societies that increasingly promote messages that we are not good enough, we must do better, look better and strive for more, resilience is crucial. But even the most resilient of people can suffer setbacks and off-days – having a positive and optimistic mindset, as well as a balanced view of the world, will help to avoid depression and despondence from taking root. Resilience keeps us focused on our goals and grateful for what we have.

The concept of being our own coach or cheerleader is a foreign one for many of us who are explicitly and implicitly told from a young age to downplay our attributes, blend in with others and criticize rather than praise ourselves. A young woman who tells her peers that she loves the way she looks is likely to receive criticism for showing off, rather than be celebrated for being positive and appreciating her body. The young woman who bemoans her weight, hair colour or body shape is far more likely to be accepted as her peers offer sympathy, words of encouragement or their own tales of image woe. This insidious process is dangerous – we are at risk of creating nations of young people who don't know how to identify and celebrate their strengths.

Although being our own best coach can be a difficult idea to conceptualize for some, it is a process worth pursuing, and can be an entirely internal endeavour, encouraging young people to develop healthy self-talk and a positive internal voice.

Being our own best coach can be described as:

- having a positive internal voice and self-talk

- the ability to put our challenges, failures and disappointments into context

- developing an optimistic mindset – seeing opportunities instead of challenges; looking for lessons and learning in 'negative' situations; believing in a positive, fulfilling world

- seeing our own potential and having aspirations

- having a sense of purpose and goals, and coaching ourselves to reach those goals

- acknowledging our talents, attributes and skills

- self-belief and the ability to build ourselves up after adversity

- being aware of our weaknesses and seeking to overcome them

- having an internal sense of guidance, ethics and principles that guides our actions to keep us on track

- listening to our mind and body and acting in our best interests.

The life coaching techniques and activities can be used by a young person wishing to address a specific issue of concern, such as poor body image or a lack of confidence, or in a more general sense, such as using coaching to stay positive, motivated, set and to reach academic or non-academic goals and so forth. For example, a young person may wish to use relaxation techniques and goal setting to deal with exam stress for a few weeks as they revise. Another young person may want to embark on a longer journey to develop confidence and friendships after relocating to a new school and struggling to settle in. This young person may wish to use specific confidence-building activities while keeping a journal to record progress.

If your children wish to use the *Life Coaching for Kids* tools to self-coach, encourage them to create a quiet space where they won't be interrupted, but to seek support if needed. Parents may wish to check in with their children to discuss any feedback and ways in which they can support their children's coaching journey, but maintaining their pace is just as crucial when self-coaching as it is in any other format.

Chapter summary

- Coaching tools can be used informally at home, to coach children one-to-one, to support whole-family goals, or for children to use unaided.

- Using coaching tools in the home can help towards creating much needed family time, and an opportunity for parents and children to connect, listen, talk and share.

- Self-coaching can help young people to develop a positive and affirmative coaching mindset, to become their own best coach.

- Be creative when using coaching techniques and activities at home – make it fun for children, and keep it short.

- Coaching techniques can be used at home for specific issues or to address specific events (for example, combating exam stress), or to generally improve children's well-being.

Part 2

The Coaching Model Explained

Chapter 7

The Coaching Mindset

The coaching relationship is unique and special, and creates an uncommon space for children and young people. Coaching provides a platform for a young person to talk, connect and share with an adult in a way that is rare – on an equal level, with respect, care, support and positive challenge. Often the relationship between adult and child is one of adult control, power and direction – usually of necessity to keep the child safe, to enable him to learn and so forth. Although coaching is not right for every child or young person, many find formal individual or group coaching to be a safe and personal space where they can express themselves and grow, without fear of ridicule, embarrassment or 'getting it wrong'.

The coaching relationship is not formed overnight, and may take time to develop and grow. The mindset of coaching is a concept that must be embedded and understood by both coach and child – so that all parties are clear about the process before they embark on a journey together. Even in informal coaching, such as a parent and child using the tools together, or a young person undertaking self-coaching, a coaching mindset helps to facilitate and create the right environment for change to occur.

The core tools and concepts used by coaches are:

- active listening
- empathy
- building rapport
- asking powerful questions
- reframing
- using skills ethically.

Active listening

Truly being listened to and heard is powerful. So often when we listen to someone else we do so passively – our focus is partly somewhere else, we are waiting for our turn to speak, or we are communicating with an agenda. Active listening creates a space for unspoken, as well as spoken, communication to take place, and helps a person to feel truly understood, valued and respected. Active listening is a skill of a good coach, and one that requires effort and practice.

Sadly the opportunities for young people to be truly listened to and heard are increasingly rare. In a classroom of 30 children and with a packed curriculum, it is difficult for the teacher to pay individual attention to each child. At home, busy schedules and constant technology can put listening to one another on the back burner. Even among children, listening to peers is not common practice – children are increasingly more likely to send a text message, or communicate via a social network site like Facebook, than speak face-to-face about an important issue.

Active listening can be described as listening on a deeper level. The 'active' part of the process describes the listener being focused, attentive and fully present, and communicating this back to the speaker. Active listening is a whole-body experience: the listener conveys that he is paying avid attention with his body language – making good eye contact, facing the speaker, leaning forward, nodding and using other signals to communicate that he is hearing both what is being said, and what is going unsaid.

Deep or active listening requires a triple focus – on what is being directly communicated; on what is not being said but is still being communicated; and a wider, intuitive sense of what is passing between speaker and listener, and is being experienced in the moment, in the environment of deep listening. Figure 7.1 illustrates the three levels of listening: surface level, deep and global listening.

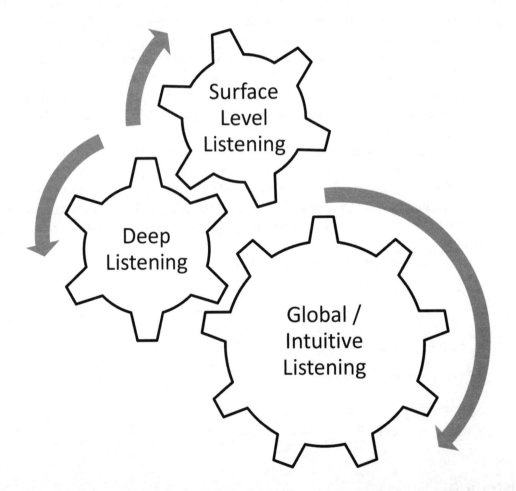

Figure 7.1: The Three Levels of Listening

SURFACE LEVEL LISTENING

- Hearing what is being directly said.

- Reflecting on the speaker's words.

- Picking up on emotion or underlying feelings if it is obvious and clear, such as an angry tone.

- Not taking note of incongruencies of speech, subtle body language or facial expressions.

- Having your own agenda – the listener is waiting to speak, asking questions for his own interest, not to help the listener reflect or build awareness, etc.

DEEP LISTENING

- Listening for more than just the words, including meaning, underlying feelings, resistance, fear, the speaker's values and beliefs and an indication of goals, listening for metaphors.

- Aware of inconsistencies.

- Reading the speaker's body language and facial expression – noticing the tone, intonation, emotive language, gestures, breathing, etc.

- The listener using non-verbal cues to demonstrate listening, such as nodding, hand gestures, leaning forward, etc.

- The listener using 'minimal encouragers' to demonstrate listening and encourage the speaker to continue, such as 'yes', 'okay', 'go on', 'mmm' and so forth.

- Using reflection and paraphrasing to communicate understanding, build empathy and to encourage the speaker to reflect on what he said.

- Using questions to clarify and provide insight and awareness.

- Using reflection and questioning to challenge the speaker to delve deeper or explore challenging thoughts and feelings to build greater awareness.

GLOBAL/INTUITIVE LISTENING

- As above; and also reading the subtle information passing between speaker and listener; having a sense of what's happening at a deeper level.

- Aware of what is underlying the words presented by the speaker; acknowledging where the emotion lies.

- Relying partly on the listener's intuition.

- Acknowledging incongruencies in the speaker's words, actions, body language, etc.

- Picking up on the energy of the speaker, and therefore the energy passing between speaker and listener; aware of shifts of energy/change of feeling in the room.

There are a number of important tools for the good, active listener. To move beyond a passive standpoint and to encourage a person to communicate and share at a deeper level (and therefore to shift his awareness or to work through difficult thoughts and feelings), a listener needs a toolkit of strategies. Asking numerous questions might get to the same conclusion, but would likely put a speaker off from wanting to share – questions can be too direct and probing, setting a person on edge or leaving him feeling interrogated.

Using reflection, paraphrasing and summarizing skills can help a speaker to feel as though he is being heard, to allow the speaker to clarify when something has not been heard or understood correctly, and to feel a sense of empathy and connection with a listener. These tools are particularly useful when working with children and young people, as they are less likely to be able to articulate themselves and provide insightful reflections on their own thoughts and feelings. A child might say 'I'm mad' when really he feels disappointed, let down or anxious.

Reflection is simply the process of reflecting or mirroring back key words, phrases or feelings to the speaker. It is not a parroting process – repeating and echoing back exactly what a person said is likely to leave him feeling annoyed and frustrated! By reflecting a word or phrase the person speaking will effectively 'offer' it back to the listener, who can then contemplate on what he himself said, and hear his own words. This helps the speaker to gain a deeper sense of how he feels, or to clarify that what he said was inaccurate and not wholly a good reflection of how he feels.

Paraphrasing and summarizing are similar tools to reflecting. They involve a longer reflection – when paraphrasing a listener will sum up a sentence or an exchange and reflect it back to a speaker. A summarization is a longer version of this, perhaps at the end of an exchange.

AN EXAMPLE OF PARAPHRASING AND SUMMARIZING

Speaker: 'I'm so mad! My parents never let me do anything I want to do!'

Listener: 'You feel mad because your parents never let you do what you want to do...'

Speaker: 'Well sometimes they let me do stuff, but they wouldn't let me go to the party on Saturday night. Everyone else was going and now I look like a loser!'

Listener: 'They sometimes let you do stuff... You feel frustrated because other people could go to the party and you couldn't. You're worried about how other people will see you now.'

Speaker: 'Yeah... I didn't really care about the party I just don't want to be the one left out. I know the other kids will be laughing at me now...'

Through a process of reflection and paraphrasing the speaker gains clarification and begins to reframe his feelings. He goes from being mad at his parents to sharing that he feels left out and is worried about how he will be perceived. The original statement about his parents not giving him any freedom was blocking the real issue. By using reflection the speaker is putting his feelings and thoughts into context – his parents don't let him do *some* things, rather than *everything*. He feels frustrated and worried about the other kids' reactions, rather than solely mad at his parents.

AN EXAMPLE OF SUMMARIZING

Speaker: 'My parents have been arguing so much, they're going to split up I just know it. And then my brother and I will be forced to choose who we live with. I hate all the arguing, I want it to stop, but I don't want them to get divorced. Why can't they just get along like adults?'

Listener: 'You feel frustrated that your parents are arguing so much, and you worry that they will get divorced. You want home to be peaceful and for everyone to get along. If your parents split up you're worried about what will happen to you and your brother.'

Summarizing is useful to bring a close to a conversation, to ensure both speaker and listener are 'on the same page' and understand what has been communicated. In coaching, summarizing can be used to ensure that client and coach both understand the focus of the session, and what the course of action is going to be.

Listening for what's unsaid

Most of us are typically used to listening and being listened to on a fairly surface level. We don't pay much attention to what is not being said, pick up on subtle incongruencies in speech, nor hear the emotion behind a person's words unless it is obvious and clear, such as someone speaking in an aggressive or angry tone. Consider a client who tells us that she is excited to be moving house and living in a new city. We hear the words and respond accordingly, telling the person how happy we are for her and what a great adventure she will have. The active listener might hear between the words, noting the speaker's deep intake of breath before she responds, or slight shrug of the shoulders. They might hear the slightly pensive tone, or note the look in her eyes, which indicate that although the move might be exciting, there are other emotions at play – perhaps she is frightened about taking such a big step, or cautious about leaving friends and family behind. The active listener hears her words, and notes the other information she is communicating, and can therefore respond on a deeper level. The active listener is making a connection with the speaker, and facilitating a space for her to share and have her feelings validated and heard.

ACTIVE LISTENING IN ACTION

Speaker: 'I'm moving home in a few weeks… Steve and I sold up and we're moving to a city a few hundred miles away… It's a big change, for sure. Exciting, though…'

Non-active listener: 'Wow! How exciting, I bet you can't wait. What an adventure!'

Active listener: 'That is a big change…a big move for you both. It must be exciting, but I imagine it must be a little daunting, too…'

Both listeners reflect on what the speaker has said, but the active listener uses the speaker's words to communicate that they have heard and understood the core of what is being said, such as 'big change'. The active listener goes a step further and reads the speaker's emotion and notes the tentativeness of her speech: the pauses and gaps between her sentences do not convey an altogether bubbly and excited person ready to make a big move. The active listener echoes this back, mirroring the same tentativeness and offering a reflection back to the speaker: 'I imagine it must be a little daunting, too.' In this way the active listener is offering a cautious suggestion, rather than an outright assumption, 'You are daunted by the move.' The speaker can then choose to refute the suggestion: 'No, I'm not daunted at all!' or meet the active listener on a more meaningful plane and choose to engage in a deeper conversation.

Speaker: 'Well yes, I suppose I am a little daunted… It is such a big move, after all. [sighs deeply] It's all happened so quickly… But I'm sure it will be fine once we get there…'

Active listener: 'It doesn't sound easy. Such a big change will take time to get used to, particularly if it's all come about quite quickly.'

The active listener uses reflection to echo the key words and phrases the speaker has used. The listener is validating the feelings of the speaker by saying that the move will take time to get used to, which helps the speaker to feel understood and to have her feelings recognized and accepted. The listener says 'It doesn't sound easy.' This conveys empathy and an appreciation for the speaker's difficult situation, which will help her to continue to explore her feelings in an honest and congruent way. Notice at this stage the listener is not asking questions, probing or delving too deeply, neither is he escalating the feeling in the conversation, such as saying 'That sounds like a nightmare! How awful for you!' The listener is keen to keep his opinions and frame of reference to himself. The speaker feels understood and safe to continue to share her thoughts and feelings.

> Speaker: 'Yes, it's been too quick, really. One minute my husband Steve was throwing the idea around; the next minute the house is on the market and he's got a new job up north, miles away from my friends and family. I've been left having to sort it all out. It's a good opportunity for him, but…' [shrugs]

At this point a good active listener is taking stock of what is going unsaid, and is reading the energy and feel of the space between them. The listener may pick up on a feeling of quiet panic, of fear and a sense of stuckness. Consider the language the speaker is using: '*throwing* the idea around', '*miles away* from my friends and family' and '*left* having to sort it all out'. Although used fairly casually in conversation, these words might convey deeper feelings. The speaker may feel backed into a corner by her husband, overpowered by his decision or desire to move. She may feel left behind, or as though her feelings and opinions about the move were left out and not considered.

A good active listener would continue to reflect, listen and gently question, to gather more information and get a better reading on how the speaker feels. As the conversation develops and the speaker feels a sense of empathy, understanding and appreciation for her situation, she will likely feel able to reveal more, and explore her thoughts and feelings – ultimately providing herself with insight and awareness that she might not have otherwise had.

Consider the difference in conversation between the standard listener and speaker, and the active listener and speaker. The first conversation is likely one we have had a million times or more, as we respond to what someone has said in the socially conventional way that is expected. The second conversation provides a unique space for the speaker to share her worries, fears and concerns, to reflect on what this move might mean for her, and to feel as though someone understands what it is like to be in her situation. She may gain insight to develop a plan of action that would help her to move forward, such as sharing her true feelings with her husband or asking him to slow the moving process down.

Coaching goes beyond just listening, to truly hearing and reading a person, creating a greater depth of communication to build insight and self-awareness.

Empathy and building rapport

Empathy is the ability to understand what someone else is feeling. What sounds simple enough is actually a complex skill, and one that is of crucial importance. Being able to place ourselves 'in someone else's shoes' is the ultimate tool to build a human connection, relationship, rapport, diminish prejudice and judgement, and build respect. This is essential in our homes, schools, communities and nations – a lack of empathy and regard for others leads to relationship breakdown, bullying, aggression, racism, abuse, and even war.

To strive to understand how it feels to live someone else's life, or to experience what they have experienced means putting ourselves in a sometimes abstract and challenging position. Feeling empathy for someone we are close to, like, or who shares our values and beliefs is far easier than feeling empathy for a person whose behaviour conflicts with our values, or who is seemingly so different to us that we struggle to understand who they are and why they do what they do.

Consider a situation where your best friend confides that she feels depressed and anxious about her weight and the way she looks. Perhaps we too have struggled with our weight and find it easy to empathize, immediately connecting with our own feelings of helplessness and frustration when dieting, and wanting our friend to feel happier and in control. Feeling and communicating empathy is fairly easy in this situation.

Now consider a child is coming to you for help because he is a persistent bully. He terrorizes other children and is physically and verbally aggressive. The child seems to feel no remorse. Imagine that you experienced pervasive bullying as a child, to the extent that the bullying taunts and scars still remain with you. Even as a now-adult, empathizing with this child may be difficult. It is hard for us to understand how the child can so ruthlessly and cruelly undermine others.

Empathy is markedly different from sympathy, and sympathy has little place in coaching. Being sympathetic, although a positive quality, can create distance between coach and client, and can devalue the client's abilities to resolve his own problems or keep him locked in a problem cycle. Figure 7.2 highlights the differences between empathy and sympathy.

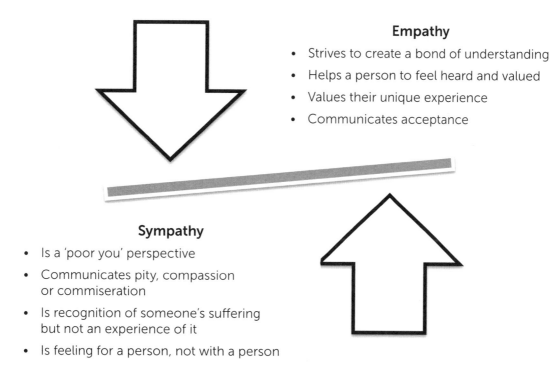

Empathy

- Strives to create a bond of understanding
- Helps a person to feel heard and valued
- Values their unique experience
- Communicates acceptance

Sympathy

- Is a 'poor you' perspective
- Communicates pity, compassion or commiseration
- Is recognition of someone's suffering but not an experience of it
- Is feeling for a person, not with a person

Figure 7.2: Empathy Versus Sympathy

Developing empathy is a lifelong process, and a skill. Finding the human qualities in us all can take time, and our empathetic skills will constantly be challenged by people who are very different to us, by our prejudices, and by our own failings – simply having a bad day and experiencing our own problems can make it difficult to empathize with someone else!

Empathy helps to build rapport and trust when coaching – rapport strengthens the relationship and helps both coach and client to feel safe, included, valued and acknowledged. Displaying empathy and rapport is essential when working with children and young people; putting their trust in an adult to share difficult thoughts, feelings and experiences can be hard for a young person. Feeling as though the adult cares and understands will help this process. A coach must use a variety of tools and strategies to communicate empathy, including active listening, paraphrasing and a reflection of the client's emotions.

Asking powerful questions

Asking questions is a natural part of conversation, and something we often do without thought. Questions provide us with information, allow us to get to the heart of a matter, or draw out someone's views on a subject. In a coaching or therapeutic scenario questioning can help to shift a client's thinking, and delve deeper into his thoughts, feelings and behaviours, providing insight and self-awareness. They can help a coach to empathize and build a connection with a client, and ultimately shift a client into a positive mindset to reach his goals.

However, questioning is a skill and requires practice. Used too sparingly and a client may feel he is talking at his coach and can lose steam. Used too frequently and a client can feel as though he is being interrogated! When asking questions the golden rule is always to consider for whose benefit the question is being asked. If it is to help the client build awareness or clarify his thoughts, it is in his best interest and of benefit. If the question is to help a coach to clarify a point the client has made, to help the coach to better help a client, then again, the question is ultimately for the client's benefit. If, however, the question is being asked because the coach is intrigued, interested or entertained, then it is likely the question is for the coach's benefit, and not the client's.

In some forms of talking therapy questions are used sparingly and with caution, but in solution-focused coaching questions can challenge clients and direct their attention, creating a shift in thinking and/or behaviour. When used correctly, questions provide clients with insight and discovery, and coaches should be mindful to allow clients time to reflect and respond, and avoid asking multiple questions in rapid succession. This 'machine gun' approach can leave clients confused, and it is likely they will only remember the last question asked, and not the preceding ones.

In life coaching both open and closed questions are used, but with empathy, care and skill. Open questions are those that invite reflection and a considered response, for example, 'How are you feeling now?' Closed questions require a limited response and can shut down a conversation, such as, 'Are you feeling angry now?' The client typically has only one of two ways to respond to this question: yes or no. This will typically require the coach to then ask another question to keep the discussion flowing. By asking an open question the coach can then use reflection skills to encourage the client to share more, such as 'You feel confused' or, 'I wonder what it's like for you to feel so frustrated.'

However, closed questions have their place. In coaching they can be used to quickly get to the heart of a matter, to be direct or to supportively challenge a client. For example, a young man is receiving coaching support to manage his anger. He has a limiting and unhelpful belief that he is an angry person, and has labelled himself as such. He feels guilty and outcast, and judges himself to be a bad person because of his anger.

Client: 'I've got anger management problems… I'm an angry kid, everyone says so.'

Coach: 'Are you always angry?'

Client: 'Yeah.'

Coach: 'Even when you're asleep?'

Client: 'Well no, obviously.'

Coach: 'What about when you're eating, or watching TV?'

Client: 'No, I'm not angry then, unless someone makes me angry.'

Coach: 'So you're angry when someone makes you feel angry.'

Client: 'Yes, I guess so.'

Although requiring a yes or no answer, the closed and direct questions challenge the client to reframe his perception of his angry feelings. There are times when he is *not* angry, and through the process of discussion and exploration he can begin to disassociate himself as a person from the emotions he experiences, realizing that they are not one and the same.

Similarly, asking 'why' questions can shut down a conversation, or may be used carefully to challenge and direct a client, as with closed questions. A bad habit used by many adults is asking children and young people 'why?' We ask why they were badly behaved, why they chose to break a rule and so forth, but usually the response is silence! Oftentimes children don't know why they do what they do; they either cannot verbalize their thought process to communicate why, or else they simply don't know what impulse caused them to act out. Asking a 'why' question can also communicate a judgement if not offered carefully. Asking 'Why are you always angry?' can leave a person feeling judged and criticized.

Coaches should also be careful not to ask leading questions without the aim of helping the client, or questions that judge or presume. When we feel we have the full picture or we have perhaps made our own conclusions about a client, our questions can convey a judgement that is inaccurate or presumptuous. Clients can either own this judgement, believing it to be true, or feel criticized, shutting down and becoming removed from the coaching relationship.

For example, a coach asks, 'How does it feel when you sabotage your efforts?' The presumption is that the client is sabotaging himself, which may or may not be true. The client may react by becoming defensive and withdrawing, firmly challenging his coach and asserting that he is not sabotaging himself. Coaching therefore becomes stuck. If a coach believed that a client might indeed be sabotaging himself, then using reflective skills would be a much gentler approach to getting to this point than asking a direct and assumptive question.

Coaches should also use deep and active listening skills to be mindful of the questions clients ask themselves. Rhetorical questions asked by the client might provide clues to the limiting beliefs and ways in which the client is holding himself back, such as, 'Why do I always mess things up?' or, 'Why am I always getting things wrong?' or 'Why do bad things always happen to me?' Coaches can explore the language clients use in their questions, such as 'always' that may give clues as to the client's frame of reference, and explore the roots of these questions in the client's beliefs about himself and the world. Unresourceful beliefs can then be challenged and worked through, to create positive, affirming alternatives.

Asking powerful questions can create shifts, and require reflection and deep thought. Powerful questions encourage us to challenge our thinking and to change our perspective, exploring when and how we came to those conclusions and challenging the validity of our thoughts. When used in a CBT model, powerful questions can help a client to explore the impact his thoughts are having on his feelings and behaviours, and therefore his life experience.

Powerful questions don't need to be complex. Often simple questions, when used appropriately, can create great shifts in thinking and attitude, such as, 'What next?'

EXAMPLES OF POWERFUL QUESTIONS

- What are you resisting?
- What would the best version of you do?
- What is the pay-off for doing 'XYZ'?
- What would be the answer if you did know?
- What are you willing to change?
- What are you not willing to change?
- What would be different if you gave yourself permission to be happy?
- What would the most confident version of you do now?
- Who do you need to be?

Powerful questions can open the mind, encourage discussion and reflection, open up the relationship and shift a person's perspective. Consider the following examples:

- If you could wave a magic wand, what would be different?
- If you could do anything your heart desired, what would you do?
- If you could be an animal, what animal would you be and why?
- If you could have a super power, what power would you have and why?
- If you woke up and your life was perfect, how would you know?
- What is the best thing about being you?
- What does the perfect life mean to you?
- What is it like to be you when you're feeling at your best?
- What is the best present you could give yourself?

Encouraging clients to ask powerful questions

Asking powerful questions is not just the role of the coach. Encouraging clients to use reflective questioning can help them to become their own best coach, and to facilitate deeper understanding, reflection and self-awareness. In particular children are not generally taught to question themselves or to develop critical thinking skills, although this is slowly gaining more prominence in education. By asking powerful questions children and young people can create a positive internal dialogue, explore the consequences to their actions and reflect on their feelings, building emotional literacy.

- How does it make me feel to be with 'X'?
- How does it make me feel to do 'XYZ'?
- I wonder what it would be like if I…?
- Is this important to me?
- What will happen next if I…?

- How will 'X' feel if I...?

- Will this make me feel good or bad?

- What is the best way forward for everyone involved?

Reframing

Human beings have a unique desire to derive meaning from the world. We constantly tell ourselves 'stories' and often create unconscious patterns of thought and behaviour to explain the world around us and to understand our place in it. In coaching, the meaning we place on something can be described as a frame – the frame provides the context for the event, situation, person or behaviour. However, the frame we place on something will significantly impact on how we respond. A positive frame creates positive feeling and results; a negative frame will likewise create a negative experience, and can feel out of our control – we feel powerless to change our experiences and results.

Just as we would put a frame around a picture to enhance or change the look of it, putting a new frame around our behaviour or thought process can shift it into a new context. Reframing, therefore, is the process of putting something in a new context, to provide a fresh perspective and to shift a client's thinking and perception. It is the process of shifting our awareness to a more resourceful, empowering standpoint.

The stories we tell ourselves (or thought patterns and beliefs we hold) can become ingrained and stuck, or can become outdated. A viewpoint that may have served us well in the past can become a negative pattern of thought that is now holding us back, such as a 'story' formed in childhood that no longer has a bearing on us as an adult. Other stories or patterns of thinking are essentially negative and have never served us well but are somehow 'stuck on repeat', creating negative feelings and cycles of poor results.

Reframing is a useful coaching tool that helps clients to see situations or to acknowledge their thoughts and feelings from a different perspective. It is more than just looking at the bright side of things or encouraging a client to think the opposite of his current thought. A clichéd and ineffective reframe pays lip service to the process of shifting perspective – reframing is a process that provides new ways for a client to consider his problems, limitations, negative experiences, thoughts and feelings, to find solutions and a positive way forward.

Being aware of a client's current frame is the first step to helping him to reframe. Clues to an unresourceful or stuck frame are provided in the client's language and themes of discussion. Unresourceful frames (or thought patterns) might be self-critical, sound disempowering, place control in someone else's hands, or generally focus on the negative, such as:

- 'I always get things wrong'

- 'I'm useless at being organized'

- 'They make me so angry'

- 'I'm too shy to make friends'

Coaches can help their clients to reframe these thoughts or behaviours to create a more positive resolution and mindset. Consider reframes of the above statements:

- 'I always get things wrong' *versus* 'I didn't get it right this time'.

- 'I'm useless at being organized' *versus* 'I am good at being spontaneous'.

- 'They make me so angry' *versus* 'I chose to let them make me feel angry'.

- 'I'm too shy to make friends' *versus* 'I'm working on becoming more confident which is helping me to meet new people'.

The reframes aren't sugar-coated examples of a perfect world scenario, but realistic reflections from a different perspective – one that perhaps the client has been unable or unwilling to see. For example, a child has been struggling to build his confidence and social skills to make friends in a new school. He feels completely disheartened when his attempt to chat to someone at lunch is ignored and brushed off. The boy feels completely rebuffed and returns to his default beliefs and thinking patterns that he is not confident, painfully shy, unable to make friends, and so forth. His coach helps to reframe the experience in a new, more empowering light. The coach highlights how far the boy has come by having the confidence to approach someone: he has demonstrated huge leaps in confidence by approaching a stranger and making conversation. The exercise wasn't a failure; the boy just needs to try approaching a different person.

Reframing is a process – assisting clients to create new, empowering stories or beliefs may take time, to ensure that old habits of thinking don't creep back in. Consider a negative thought pattern or belief that you've held for a long time – it is likely that the roots of the thought aren't clear. You can't remember when you started thinking that thought, or when you decided to believe it to be true, but at some point, or over a period of time, the thought was repeated often enough, or enough power and credence was given to it, that it became cemented as a belief. We don't often challenge our thoughts or beliefs – they are taken as fact.

The intrinsic belief 'I am not a confident person' is generally a negative one. It wouldn't serve a person well, in the main, to believe himself to not be confident. Asking someone to suddenly believe he is confident probably won't do the trick. However, by examining situations and thoughts from a new context, providing a different perspective and looking for the evidence to support this new perspective, clients can begin to create new, empowering beliefs that will produce better results. This process is explored further in Chapter 11 when discussing CBT and NLP tools.

Using skills ethically

The most important concept for a coach or any adult working with young people to embody is that of working ethically and safely. Ethics describe the moral principles held by a person whose intent is to help and not harm. Our ethics place the client at the centre of the coaching relationship, and ensure we are working appropriately, within the client's best interests. Working ethically means leaving our judgements, preconceptions and prejudices at the door, and being present and open to hearing the client. Loosely, being ethical can be described as 'doing the right thing', although in practice this can be challenging. Ultimately, a coach sets an example and is a role model for a child or young person (as every adult is), whether aware of it or not.

An ethical coach will:

- have a positive intention

- be working for the benefit of the child, not for the coach's own interest or curiosity

- maintain confidentiality (where appropriate)

- be working within the coach's level of proficiency (that is, not working beyond his level of training or understanding, and instead referring a client on to someone with greater or more specialized expertise)

- act as guide and supporter, not expert or advice-giver

- commit to his own professional development

- refer and adhere to policies and procedures, including an ethical framework if appropriate, school behaviour policies, and so forth.

Chapter summary

- The core concepts for life coaching are active listening, empathy and building rapport, asking powerful questions, reframing and using skills ethically.

- Deep or active listening involves listening for more than just the words, including meaning, underlying feelings, resistance, fear, the speaker's values and beliefs and an indication of goals.

- Empathy is the ability to understand what someone else is feeling and communicate an understanding. It helps to build rapport and trust with clients.

- Powerful questions encourage us to challenge our thinking and change our perspective, exploring when and how we came to those conclusions and challenging the validity of our thoughts.

- Reframing is a useful coaching tool that helps clients to see situations or to acknowledge their thoughts and feelings from a different perspective.

- The most important concept for a coach or any adult working with young people to embody is that of working ethically and safely.

Chapter 8

Goal Setting

Goal setting is a key action of life coaching, helping people to move forward with purpose and clarity to create life-affirming changes. The concept of setting and reaching goals is not an unusual one – each day we set and accomplish objectives, however small, whether as a conscious effort or not. Without setting and reaching goals our lives can become aimless, apathetic and devoid of meaning.

There are three stages to reaching a goal: setting the goal, working towards it and accomplishment. Each stage comes with its own rewards and challenges. The initial process of setting a goal can create a sense of purpose, excitement, anticipation and focus, although for some people this can be the most difficult part – narrowing their focus to just one goal, or believing in themselves to be able to commit to setting a goal in the first place. For others, the act of working towards their target provides the most benefit. They feel rewarded by noting the milestones they've reached, or by seeing the changes in their life. The act of working towards an ambition can shift a person's perspective of life. However, maintaining focus and the determination to continue can be difficult, particularly when results plateau or the object of our desires seems a long way off.

Overall, accomplishing a goal often provides us with both external and internal rewards. A person may experience a sense of pride, triumph and empowerment, increased self-worth, self-confidence and purpose. She may have realized tangible rewards, such as financial gain, or intangible benefits, such as developing new skills and attributes, either in the process of reaching her goal (such as staying focused, organized or determined) or in the completion of the target, such as learning the skill of mastering a new recipe or writing a novel.

Goals come in all shapes and sizes, both specific and/or time-limited (such as wanting to run a marathon), and ongoing (such as wanting to be healthy and to exercise regularly). In essence, the effort given to reach a goal gives our lives a sense of purpose. In life coaching clients are supported to set and reach goals to promote positive change and action, using a solution-focused approach. Without the element of goal setting coaching can slip into the realms of other talking therapies, focused on the clients' problems, or might leave a client going around in circles, knowing how she wants her life to change but not knowing how to make those changes a reality.

Basics of goal setting

There are numerous books, resources and websites that provide advice about goal setting. In today's action-oriented, always-connected world the internal and external pressure to be doing more, achieving more, earning more and so on, is challenging and sometimes draining. In our own lives we may have felt the pressure to get the next promotion, to sign up for a marathon because our friends have, to lose weight to look like the people on the magazine covers, to move to a bigger house, own a better car, and so on. This pressure can be exaggerated by looking into the windows to other people's lives that may encourage us to compare ourselves unfavourably with others. This is true for children and young people, too, who feel the pressure to achieve better grades at school, become more popular, develop a talent like the people they see on TV, be prettier and more attractive to the opposite sex, and so on. In the rush to complete someone else's goals we can lose sight of what it is that drives us and makes us happy.

Setting and reaching goals should therefore be a positive urge to create fulfilment and intrinsic well-being. A coach should be aware of the underlying drivers and motives for a person's goal, to ensure that the person's ambition is within her own best interest. Trying to accomplish something for the wrong reasons will either fall flat of success, or once achieved, not bring the desired reward, leaving the person deflated, frustrated or confused as to why her effort hasn't delivered the feelings of satisfaction and happiness expected.

Some people will come to coaching with a very specific idea of what they want to achieve. Others will come with a 'shopping list' of objectives and ambitions that may take a lifetime to fulfil! For some people, their goal is hardly a goal at all, just a vague sense that something needs to change, such as 'I want to be happier.'

When coaching children and young people there is a greater likelihood that their goals will be broad and unspecific – 'I just want the bullying to stop' or 'I want to be prettier' – or alternatively, their objectives for coaching will be non-existent, having not understood what coaching is all about, or not being able to articulate what they wish to change in their life.

Working with vague goals

The first step to setting goals can be summed up in the common acronym, SMART, which stands for:

Specific

Measurable

Attainable

Realistic

Timely or **T**ime-limited

Being *specific* helps to keep the goal more manageable and to ensure that you know when and how it will be accomplished, and therefore helps to create a plan of action. A broad, vague goal of wanting to be healthier is a good concept, but without being specific the person may not know how to start taking steps towards reaching this aim, nor will she know when she has achieved it! How do you define becoming 'healthy'? The concept is so wide that the person could be left failing to take a first step forward, or conversely, pulled in a dozen different directions trying diets, workouts, weight lifting, healthy eating regimes and other practices that may be near impossible to keep up.

The process of specifying goals can help to ensure that the person really wants what she's setting out to achieve. Consider the following example, starting with an initial, vague goal, and moving towards a more specific plan of action:

Goal 1: To be happier.

Goal 2: To be happier at work.

Goal 3: To enjoy going to work each day by feeling more fulfilled.

Goal 4: To do work that makes me feel fulfilled.

Goal 5: To do less cold-call selling and to build relationships with customers.

The initial goal was so broad and all-encompassing, and far too vague. By focusing on the initial goal the client could have been taken on a completely different tangent, focusing instead on her health or home life: she actually wanted to feel happier about her job and gain more fulfilment through her work. Through the process of narrowing down the goal to something more specific the coach could ask questions such as, 'What makes you feel fulfilled?' or 'What could be different at work so you would enjoy going there?' to help the client zone in on her true aims. The final goal might be something along the lines of 'To find a job that utilizes my skills of relationship-building and other talents'.

When setting goals in any context, the SMART acronym helps to ensure they are more likely to be reached.

Goals also need to be *measurable* and *attainable*. Providing a way for progress to be measured allows clients to evaluate their success, make any changes to their plan of action and attain their goal effectively. Having the necessary attitude and determination to reach a goal also makes it attainable, setting a client up for success.

Finally, making goals *realistic* and *timely* are the last pieces to the success puzzle. Whether a client can reach her goal is completely dependent on the individual, the support she has, external circumstances or blocks that appear, and the suitability of the goal for the person's needs and what she is capable of achieving. Lastly, setting a realistic timeframe for achievement will allow a client to track her progress, and ensure small steps add up to overall success. Often we can overestimate what we are capable of achieving in short periods such as a day or one week, and underestimate what we can achieve in a longer period, such as a month or year.

For example, a young woman wishes to be healthy and lose weight but rarely exercises at present. Her goal is to go to the gym every day and to lose ten pounds in a month. She has never stepped foot inside a gym before, and chose the weight loss goal because she'd seen it written on the front of a magazine in relation to a celebrity who had crash-dieted to lose the same amount of weight. It is unlikely that this young woman's goals are attainable in their current form. She may well enjoy the gym, or be able to lose ten pounds, but making her first aims more realistic and attainable will ensure she doesn't fall at the first hurdle.

However, this is not to say that the only realistic goals are small and inconsequential, or that reaching a significant, monumental goal isn't achievable. Earning a PhD, for example, is an extremely worthwhile goal, but one that needs to start with passing secondary school, getting a Bachelor's degree, a Master's degree and so forth. By setting and accomplishing smaller goals we become spurred on to move towards greater achievements, knowing that we are capable and have the necessary skills for success. As we achieve greater goals our perception of the world can shift – what we thought of as impossible becomes altogether more feasible.

Working with a shopping list of goals

Some people come to coaching with a veritable shopping list of objectives. Rather than a vague notion of what needs to be changed, they are armed with a desire to change almost every aspect of their lives at once. Having too many goals can lead to paralysis and overall inaction as a person struggles to know what to focus on first, or flits from one target to another. Having a 'shopping list' of goals can also be a way of avoiding taking action – the client wants to change everything and becomes so overwhelmed she does nothing. Helping a client to focus on one goal at a time will ensure that she doesn't hide behind her goals, allowing a fear of change or a lack of self-belief to inhibit her progress.

The 'shopping list' approach can also be an indication of a person unwilling to let herself be happy and find pleasure. The constant pursuit of greater and greater ambition can be driven by ego, low self-esteem or childhood conditioning – the person is in constant pursuit of trying to make someone else happy, or to belie a lack of self-belief. She gains no pleasure or satisfaction in attaining a goal, but just feels a constant pressure to be better, do more, and move on to the next thing, in an exhausting cycle of perfection. An indication of this might be found in the person's language that may be littered with 'shoulds' – for example, this person might say phrases such as, 'I should be doing "XYZ" by now' or 'I should be earning more.'

Working with non-existent goals

It is likely that some children and young people will come to coaching with no idea of what needs to be changed in their life. The concept of having power and control over our lives to effect change is a fairly abstract one, and goal setting is not something we typically encourage young people to do, aside from reaching academic goals or passing exams. Young people can feel powerless to change their life circumstances because typically they are not in control of large portions of their day-to-day existence – they have to attend school, do what they're told to by parents, live where they are told to, and so forth. Certainly, some aspects of their lives will be predetermined or fixed. However, helping a child to acknowledge what they *can* change, and explore how to change the way they respond to permanent situations, will create a shift in outlook and life experience. Above all, the process of setting and reaching goals is empowering, and builds lifelong skills and awareness.

Using a tool such as the Wheel of Life or General Scaling Tool (found in Part 3) can help if a child or young person comes to coaching without a clear idea of a goal. These activities can help the young person to pinpoint the main areas of her life that are impacting on her well-being, or help to identify the actions she needs to take to achieve a better mental state, such as feeling happier or more confident.

Determining the validity of goals

Checking the validity of goals refers to identifying whether a person is setting a goal for the right reasons. It is crucial to spend time identifying why a person wants to achieve something, to ensure it supports her well-being and is in her best interests. It is easy to fall into the trap of starting something in the right way, for all the wrong reasons, and this can be a highly unconscious process. We may have felt the pressure of going for a promotion, to have a child, or to return to studying, because of a perceived or real external pressure. It might have seemed the 'right thing to do' or what I 'should' be doing. Perhaps the pressure was placed on us by a spouse or parent who misguidedly felt that it would be the right thing for us.

It is easy to get caught up in someone else's ideas and for their goals to become our own. A person may want to achieve the goal on one level and may sound quite convincing in her pursuit of her aim, but underlying this drive is someone else's agenda, low self-esteem or negative beliefs. A person is far more likely to be motivated to reach her goal, and to receive pleasure and satisfaction from it, if it is valid and driven by her own passions and desires.

Imposed goals can come from both external sources and internal negative beliefs. Consider the child whose whole focus is centred on academic achievement to get a place at a good university, despite her passion for the arts and music. Or the child who is following her father's footsteps to undertake a career in medicine, despite finding the pursuit of the career utterly miserable. These children might be trying to please a parent and gain their approval; they may be directly or indirectly pushed towards the goal by the parent who wants to see their own dreams fulfilled through the child; or may be spurred on by unresourceful beliefs and messages they received from key role models, such as 'You're not good enough to be a doctor' or 'You'll never amount to anything.'

Negative internal beliefs can unconsciously drive a person's life if left unchecked. These beliefs are likely formed in childhood and adolescence, and can become ingrained, influencing a person's outlook on life, and therefore her thoughts, feelings, behaviours and interactions with others. A child who was repeatedly told (directly or indirectly), 'We love you as you are', 'We believe in you', 'You're a wonderful person' and so forth will likely have a different outlook than a child who received messages such as, 'You're not good enough', 'You're a waste of space' or 'You'll never amount to anything.' This is not to say that every person who explicitly or subconsciously received such messages will create negative beliefs and suffer under their weight. Developing self-awareness and becoming conscious of our drivers will help to eradicate unresourceful beliefs and create a life driven by self-affirming thoughts and values.

Consider the beliefs we build about life ourselves that can become ingrained, such as:

- The world is not a safe place.

- People can't be trusted.

- People are out to get you.

- I need to be self-sufficient.

- Showing emotion is weak.

- Being independent isn't feminine.

- I must be in control.

- I can't ask for help; needing help is a weakness.

When coaching a child or young person be mindful of the language they use that might indicate that the validity of their goal isn't sound. Phrases such as 'I should', 'I must' or 'I need to' are potentially warning lights to goals that are driven by negative beliefs, low self-esteem or someone else's agenda, such as:

- I should work harder at school.

- I need to be stronger.

- I should be the perfect son/daughter.

- I must lose weight to be more attractive to others.

- I need to be more confident so others will like me.

- I should fight back/I need to be more aggressive.

- I should be like the other girls/boys.

Spending time working through a child's goal will help to pinpoint negative drivers, and identify the impact and purpose of reaching the goal. Is it to make the child happy, or someone else? Will the child's life be enriched by achieving this goal? Coaches should ask questions to gain insight and to help the child build self-awareness, such as:

- 'Supposing you went home today and that goal had been reached. What would be different?'

- 'Who will notice if you reach that goal? What would their reaction be?'

- 'What will happen next?'

- 'How will others know you've changed?'

- 'How will you feel inside?'

- 'If you reach this goal, who will be the person who gains the most?' or 'Who will get the most out of it?'

Sometimes children come to coaching with an implausible and unsound goal that is clearly driven by negative beliefs or a skewed perception of what's in their best interests. As a caring adult our instinct might be to quickly disapprove of their objectives and put them on a much healthier, empowering route, or to disregard their thoughts completely. How often do we say to a child, 'Don't be silly, you're not tired!' or 'You don't want to give up tennis, you love it!' These sorts of responses are easily given, and although often provided with the best intentions, can close down an exchange, discrediting the child's feelings.

For example, a young woman declares that she wants to lose weight to be more attractive to the opposite sex. Our instinct is to tell her she doesn't need to do it; she is beautiful as she is, and so forth. While this may well be true, this doesn't help the young woman to understand the roots of her goal, nor does it help her to challenge her negative beliefs and perceptions. More likely our good intentions will serve to invalidate her feelings, disempower her, and leave her feeling unsupported. Instead, undertaking a process of exploration of the goal and the underlying thoughts and feelings can help to build her self-awareness and come to a more positive conclusion. For example:

Client: 'I need to lose weight. I want to be thinner and prettier.'

Coach: 'Okay. Tell me more.'

Client: 'Well I need to be a size 6. The boys will like me if I'm smaller.'

Coach: 'So you want to lose weight so the boys will like you?'

Client: 'Yes. Boys don't like big girls.'

Coach: 'Do you think you're a big girl?'

Client: 'No, not big…well maybe. My thighs are too big. I need to exercise more or lose weight or something.'

Coach: 'So if you were thinner what would happen next?'

Client: 'The boys would notice me.'

Coach: 'Is that what you want, for the boys to notice you?'

Client: 'Yeah. Well, not just the boys, the girls too. I want people to see me and think I'm pretty, not just ignore me.'

Coach: 'You want people to notice and appreciate you.'

Client: 'Yes. I want people to like me.'

Coach: 'Do you like people because they're thin?'

Client: 'No. I like them because they're nice.'

Coach: 'So you like people because they're nice, but you want people to like you because you're thin?'

Client: 'Well, no. I just want people to like me.'

Coach: 'Would it be fair to say that your goal is to be appreciated by others?'

Client: 'Yes. I don't have any friends in this school. I just want to be noticed.'

Coach: 'So something we could work on in coaching is helping you to make new friends?'

Client: 'Yes, that's exactly it.'

It is important to check the ecology of the goal – the overall impact of the goal on the person's life, her well-being and those around her. An unecological goal will have unwanted 'side-effects' for the person and/or others. In the above example the girl could lose lots of weight, endanger her health, develop risky behaviours to gain the attention of the opposite sex, or ultimately still find herself isolated at school, despite having gone to the effort of losing lots of weight and achieving something she thought would make a big difference to her life.

Chunking goals

When a positive, valid and ecological goal has been defined, the next step is often to 'chunk it down'. Chunking goals refers to the process of turning large objectives into smaller, manageable pieces to ensure success. For example, the leap from secondary school to gaining a PhD is too great for almost anyone to imagine or reach; the step from a Master's programme to a PhD seems far more manageable and achievable. Without the steps in between the overall goal of obtaining a PhD seems completely unrealistic or 'pie in the sky'. By focusing on one step at a time a person is supported along a journey without falling at the first hurdle or being put off by not experiencing immediate success. Chunking goals can also keep people on track, so they don't lose enthusiasm along the way. For example:

Overall goal: To lose 25 pounds in weight.

Chunked goals: To join a gym.

To create a healthy eating plan.

To eat three pieces of fruit and vegetables a day.

To be able to walk non-stop for 20 minutes, three times a week.

To be able to run non-stop for 5 minutes, three times a week.

To try one new fitness class at the gym.

To be able to run non-stop for 15 minutes, three times a week.

The chunked goals can be added as the client progresses. The first step towards the goal of losing a significant amount of weight might be joining a gym, or it could be walking around the neighbourhood each evening. These are small, easy manageable steps that can be added to and developed. As the client becomes more confident and is reaching her smaller goals, she can add another chunk, for example, running instead of walking, or trying a fitness class. A client can mark her success along the way, in terms of weight loss, achievement of the smaller goals, and so forth.

Chunking goals can be particularly helpful for children and young people, to keep their overall objectives in perspective and to stay on track. Children are less able to conceptualize and project themselves far into the future than adults, so focusing on smaller achievements in the near future may help.

The next step in goal setting is creating an action plan to guide and measure progress. Without having a clear plan of action this process can become vague or a person can become lost along the way. The plan outlines the 'chunked' goals, and provides detail as to how those targets will be met. As with all processes in coaching, creating an action plan needs to be client-led. The plan will need to be simple, easy to understand and easy to remember, in a language that the client can grasp. Ideally an action plan should be visual – a written or drawn account that the client can keep and refer back to. (An action planning pro forma is included in Part 3 of *Life Coaching for Kids*.)

Feedback versus failure

Failure, or fear of failure, can be the biggest hurdle to achieving a goal. Depending on a person's connotations with failure, sometimes the perception and imagined thought of failing is enough to stop the person from trying. From a young age the concept of failing is tied to a host of negative thoughts and feelings, including shame, guilt, not being good enough, letting themselves and others down, punishment, and so forth. For children, failure might be a regular experience that creates a mindset of 'why bother?'

Reframing the idea of failure into feedback can shift a person's perspective and provide the impetus to keep going. The process of failing is how we learn – we aren't born knowing how to talk, walk, play computer games or read books. By trial and error we eventually come to master each activity, and move on to the next. When failure becomes coupled with disapproval, punishment and shame, the process becomes one of right or wrong, not of feedback and progression.

Using each 'failure' as feedback helps to measure progress towards goals, and identify what needs to be changed, improved or strengthened to reach success. The feedback contains learning, which will help towards future success. The process of 'failing' becomes empowering and manageable, and stops a person from becoming put off. Consider the following example with a young boy whose anxieties are creating trouble with him falling and staying asleep at night.

Client: 'I tried to sleep but I had a nightmare! And then I couldn't get back to sleep again afterwards. It's no good, I can't do it!'

Coach: 'So you managed to fall asleep, but when you did, you had a nightmare?'

Client: 'Yes. It's no good; I'll never be able to sleep again.'

Coach: 'A few weeks ago you were having a lot of trouble falling asleep, and now you're managing to do it quite easily.'

Client: 'Yeah I guess, but I still keep waking up.'

Coach: 'Okay. So what's helped you to fall asleep recently?'

Client: 'Using those relaxation ideas you showed me.'

Coach: 'Great, so what have you learned?'

Client: 'I've learned how to relax to fall asleep.'

Coach: 'That sounds like a big step forward from when we started! So what do we need to focus on next?'

Client: 'Being able to go back to sleep if I wake up I guess.'

Coach: 'I wonder if you could use some of those relaxation ideas if you wake up in the night?'

Client: 'I guess I could try that...'

Through a process of taking stock, evaluating progress and using the 'failure' to determine where to focus next, the child begins to realize how far he has come, the skills he has available to him, and the next step on his journey.

Setting goals with children and young people

Working with children and young people to set and reach their goals is not an exact science, and will be a journey for both child and coach. Following the process below can ensure goal setting is as successful and rewarding as possible. Coaches should also be flexible – goals may change or develop through the coaching process. Be mindful to keep goals and action plans simple, and to make it a fun, positive process, helping young people to understand the skills they are learning along the way. Figure 8.1 summarizes the goal-setting process, from defining the goal, to reviewing progress.

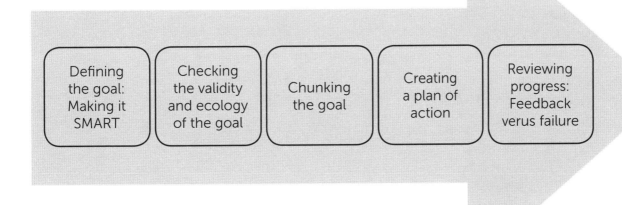

Figure 8.1: The Goal Setting Process

Chapter summary

- Keep goals SMART: Specific, Measurable, Attainable, Realistic and Timely.
- Avoid vague goals and 'shopping lists' that may indicate avoidance or fear.
- Make sure goals are valid and support the child's well-being.
- Break large goals down into smaller chunks.
- Keep track of progress and highlight how so-called 'failures' can be useful feedback.

Chapter 9

Challenging Negative Core Beliefs

Our beliefs and values form the cornerstones of what it means to be us. They shape our experience of the world, how we think and process our thoughts, how we respond to situations and how we interact with others. Our beliefs can be described as the filter through which we view the world.

Our core beliefs are often formed in childhood and adolescence, shaped by early experiences that became ingrained in our mind, either through repetition or the strength with which the experience impacted on us. A belief is, in essence, no more than a thought pattern. The importance we place on a thought or the strength we give it determines the level of impact it has on our lives. Beliefs can be both positive and negative, such as holding a belief at our core that we are good, worthy of success and happiness. This is likely to impact on our lives in a variety of positive ways, and when setbacks and problems occur (as they undoubtedly will), our core beliefs will underpin our thought processes and shape our actions. Perhaps we suffer a bad romantic break-up that leaves us feeling wounded and distrustful: despite experiencing the expected feelings of hurt, upset and frustration, eventually our core beliefs will win out, and we will explain the break-up to ourselves in a positive and optimistic light, such as thinking the person wasn't right for us, we will meet someone else soon, we can be happy alone, and so forth.

For the person who has a negative core belief, such as believing he is a bad person, unworthy of happiness and deserving of misery, such a setback as a bad relationship break-up would likely invoke a far more negative explanation. His core beliefs will produce thoughts and feelings that connect the current situation with his negative self-perception, and he may explain the break-up in terms of 'It was only a matter of time', 'I am unlovable' or 'It must have been my fault.'

Our core beliefs can be difficult to identify. They often exist in the subconscious mind, and are so ingrained that, far from being just thoughts we have given weight to, they appear to be undeniable truths. Core beliefs can be insidious – our conscious mind is unlikely to constantly replay thoughts about us being a bad person. In fact it may be a thought that rarely passes through our mind from day to day. Instead, the core belief might be triggered when something bad happens, or may slip into our everyday experience in far more sneaky ways, such as through our internal voice or decision making.

The data or messages gathered from our early interactions, key role models and significant life experiences form our core beliefs, which can become triggered at any time. A person can then add even further credence to the belief, finding new evidence to support it. In the example above, the person's belief that he is a bad person is triggered by his partner ending the relationship. This person views the experience through the lens of his beliefs, adding it to the bank of 'proof' that he is a bad and unworthy person. The person is locked in this mindset and the cycle is complete. Figure 9.1 illustrates this cycle.

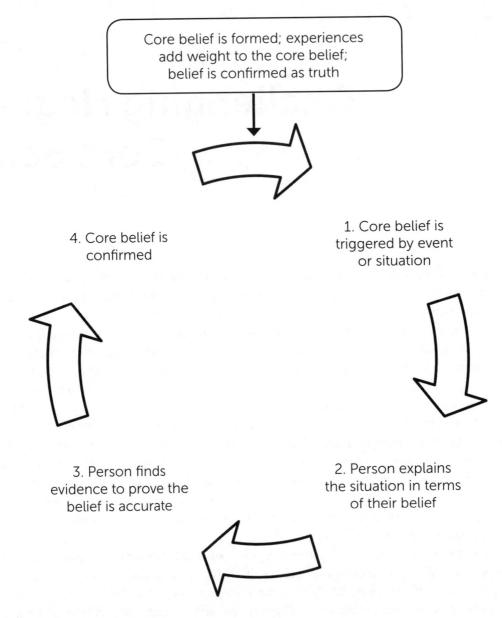

Figure 9.1: The Cycle of Core Beliefs

Identifying limiting beliefs

When core beliefs have a negative impact on a person's life and well-being they can be described as 'limiting'. Limiting beliefs stop people from truly experiencing life, feeling good about themselves, trying new things and attaining their goals. Although just a pattern of thought, a limiting core belief can hold significant sway over a person – it is his interpretation of reality and it might have become so ingrained that the opposite seems unthinkable.

Core beliefs can be based on thoughts that were appropriate and true at some time or another, in relation to a specific circumstance, place, person or situation. They become problematic when they become 'blanket' assumptions by which all circumstances, places, people or situations are measured. Consider a child being raised in a highly chaotic, unstable home. The father is physically violent and the mother is verbally abusive. The neighbourhood the child lives in is highly dangerous and crime-ridden. This child creates a thought process that 'people are out to get me', which in his immediate circumstance might well be true, to some extent. There is a degree of usefulness about this thought in his current state: although a negative perception, it may help the child to be careful when walking through his neighbourhood, or to avoid his father when he has been drinking alcohol, for example.

However, when the child turns this thought into a belief and takes it into a different circumstance, it becomes limiting and negative, such as when he starts a new school, or when he is older and starts a career, as illustrated in Figure 9.2.

Limiting beliefs can be identified in a young person's pattern of thinking and language. They may be repeated often, in various guises, or be described in absolutes, such as 'everyone is out to get me' or 'no one cares about me'.

EXAMPLES OF LIMITING BELIEFS

- 'I am stupid' *or* 'I'm no good at school' *or* 'I can't be successful'

- 'I am unlovable' *or* 'No one likes me'

- 'I am unworthy' *or* 'I don't deserve happiness/success/love etc.'

- 'The world is an unsafe place'

- 'I can't trust others' *or* 'People are out to get me' *or* 'People let you down'

- 'I have to be in control'

- 'I am not confident' *or* 'I am shy' *or* 'I can't make friends'

- 'I am unattractive'

- 'I am too bossy'

- 'I must be perfect'

Some of the above beliefs may be gateways to core beliefs, for example, a young woman might believe she has to be perfect at everything she does, which substantiates a core belief of not being good enough. Multiple beliefs can exist around a central theme, such as 'I'm stupid', 'I'm not good enough' or 'I can't be successful.'

When coaching a child or young person it may be useful to keep a note of any phrases mentioned that sound like limiting beliefs. This can help to form a picture of where the child is being held back. CBT techniques can help to challenge negative beliefs and reframe current situations with positive thoughts. (These techniques are explored further in Chapter 11.)

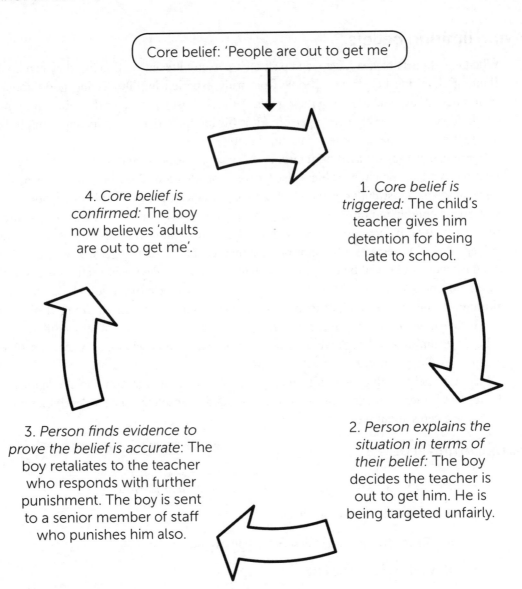

Figure 9.2: A Child's Limiting Belief

Challenging core beliefs

Consider a positive belief you hold about yourself: you are a good person; you are loved; you are capable of succeeding at anything you set your mind to. Think about the way this belief impacts on your life – how it has helped you to grow, challenged you, or helped you in tough times. Now, imagine if someone tried to convince you of the opposite. How would that feel? Would you try and hold on to your belief?

Although the process of helping children to reframe their beliefs and choose more empowering patterns of thought is undoubtedly positive, as coaches and caring adults we must be mindful of how challenging this can be. A belief, however negative, might be a completely normal way of seeing the world for a child who knows no different and has conditioned himself to think in those terms. It is crucial to proceed with care and consideration of this.

However, children are typically more adept at challenging, reframing and changing their beliefs, which are typically less ingrained than adults' patterns of thinking. Adults will have far more experience of repeating and finding evidence to support their core beliefs than children.

Challenging unhelpful and damaging core beliefs will take time and patience. It is a process of support, encouragement and guidance using strategies both in coaching and between sessions or after coaching has ended. Encouraging young people to learn and use the strategies on their own will help to build lifelong skills and awareness that can be used to challenge future unhelpful patterns of thinking as they arise.

Strategies to challenge negative beliefs

IDENTIFYING THE PAY-OFFS (OR GAINS) FOR HOLDING ONTO THE BELIEF, VERSUS THE COSTS

In child-friendly language this might be described as 'What might be the reasons why I would want to believe this to be true? What might be the reasons why I wouldn't want to believe this to be true?' It is usually helpful to start with the reasons why the child wouldn't want to believe it first, before looking at the pay-offs. This can be a difficult idea to conceptualize and may take some time to unpick and explore.

For example, belief of 'I am stupid':

Reasons why I don't want to believe this to be true: 'I feel bad when I think I'm stupid'; 'It stops me from trying'; 'I'm always comparing myself to other people'; 'I don't ask for help in case people think I'm stupid, too'

Reasons why I might want to believe this is true: 'Sometimes I don't have to try things I'm frightened of'; 'People sometimes feel sorry for me'; 'I can use it as an excuse when I don't try hard enough or don't bother to study at school'

Identifying pay-offs versus costs can be challenging and might be better suited to older young people. (An activity to use this process in coaching can be found in Part 3.)

FINDING THE EVIDENCE TO SUPPORT THE BELIEF

This is a process of finding the evidence to prove the belief is true, versus the evidence to disprove the belief, looking back at the child's past experiences. This process should challenge and invalidate the child's negative beliefs. In child-friendly terms this might be explained as, 'Can you think of times when something happened to make you think this was true? Can you think of times when something happened to make you think it wasn't true?'

For example, belief of 'I am not a confident person':

Times when I thought this was true: 'When I started school and found it difficult to go and chat to people'; 'When I forgot my lines in the school play and turned red in front of everyone'; 'When the teacher asked me to solve the algebra equation in class and I didn't know what to say'

Times when I thought this wasn't true: 'When I made a joke in class and everyone laughed'; 'When I got an award for writing stories and had to stand in front of the whole school to receive it'; 'When I went out with my friends wearing a new outfit that suited me'

IDENTIFY A POSITIVE BELIEF, SUCH AS 'I CAN BE CONFIDENT'

Initially, a child might need some help and coaxing to challenge the 'evidence' for his negative belief. The child in the above example believes he is unconfident because he forgot his lines in the school play. However, this can be reframed to a more positive conclusion – it takes significant confidence to sign up to be in a play, to stand on stage in front of an audience, and so forth. Through this process the belief can be reframed as 'I am not confident in some situations' which is a much more manageable thought than an absolute label of being an unconfident person. With this reframed belief the coach and child can focus on how to develop the child's confidence in the situations he finds most difficult – a far easier undertaking – and slowly identify and incorporate a new, empowering belief in his life, 'I can be confident.'

GRADING THE BELIEF WITH A PERCENTAGE RATING

This process involves listing all the evidence that disproves the belief is not 100 per cent true, that is, anything that suggests there is even a shadow of doubt that the belief might be true. This will likely be a long list!

- **Step 1:** Identify the percentage rating, from 1–100 per cent, that describes how true the belief is for the child initially, with 100 per cent being completely true, and 1 per cent being barely true at all. For example, 'I believe I am stupid – 99 per cent'

- **Step 2:** List all the evidence that disproves the belief, for example, the coach asks, 'What are some of the ways in which you're not stupid? What are you good at?'

- **Step 3:** Give the belief a new percentage rating, based upon the new information, for example, 'I believe I am stupid – 45 per cent'

- **Step 4:** Identify what would help to take that belief from the current percentage to a lower percentage. For example, the coach might ask, 'What thoughts would you need to think to turn that 45 per cent down to 40 per cent?'

- **Step 5:** Identify a new, empowering belief that matches the new percentage rating, for example, 'I am good at some things' or 'I am okay'

Activities to challenge negative beliefs and create positive thought processes can be found in Part 3 of *Life Coaching for Kids*.

Chapter summary

- Beliefs are just thought processes, repeated and ingrained.

- Beliefs can be positive and negative.

- Beliefs shape our experience of life and are used to measure and interpret the world around us.

- We find 'evidence' to support our beliefs.

- Negative core beliefs can be challenged and reframed into positive and affirming viewpoints.

Chapter 10

The Mind–Body Connection

The mind and body are inextricably linked: good physical health impacts upon our mental state, and vice versa. When we are in pain, suffering an illness, or just feel 'under the weather' it can be hard to maintain a positive mental state. Similarly, when we are troubled, stressed or anxious our physical being is often impacted – we have difficulty sleeping, experience headaches, feel sluggish, worn out, low in energy, and so on.

On a different level, our internal or mental state directly affects our behaviour, which in turn affects our physical well-being. Negative emotional states can lead people to:

- self-medicate with alcohol, food, drugs or develop an over-reliance on other coping mechanisms

- develop eating disorders

- self-harm

- engage in risky or unbalanced behaviour

- attempt suicide.

Life coaching supports a person's whole well-being, including both the physical and mental state. Given the interconnectedness of our bodies one element cannot be taken in isolation. Coaching can help to provide balance and to promote a healthy and positive internal state, which in turn can help to create a better physical state.

Positive and negative thinking

The quality of our thoughts determine the quality of our lives – having a positive outlook can help us to keep problems in perspective and to avoid becoming stuck or falling at the first hurdle when things don't go our way. Research conducted into optimism and learned helplessness found that having an optimistic outlook and way of explaining the world to ourselves can stop us from feeling helpless. In his ground-breaking book *Learned Optimism*, Martin Seligman writes, 'An optimistic explanatory style stops helplessness, whereas pessimistic explanatory style spreads helplessness' (1991, p.15). Seligman stated that pessimism is an entrenched habit of the mind that can lead to depression, underachievement, and even poor health (1995).

Life coaching can help people to develop a positive perspective and to challenge negative patterns of thought that no longer serve them well. However, this is not about just looking on the bright side of things or expecting 'sunshine and rainbows'. This simplistic view won't work for many people, particularly those experiencing challenging circumstances or with a traumatic past. Telling a child who is being viciously bullied to 'think positively' is condescending, naive, and potentially harmful. Life has its challenges, and it is natural to feel negative from time to time. But it is the way in which we interpret, explain and respond to life events that determines their overall impact.

Given that life coaching helps people to create positive change, the process of replacing negative patterns of thought that reinforce negative beliefs is important. This process can be achieved in a variety of ways but will take time. It is important that the shift from negative to neutral or positive is genuine. Encouraging a young person to deny or suppress her negative thoughts or feelings is not the answer. If a child is being bullied she has a right to feel anger, fear, depression or powerlessness, and coaching may be the only place she feels safe enough to share those feelings. Coaches also need to be mindful for a sudden change in attitude that might indicate that a child is trying to please them or gain approval by pretending everything is 'all better now'.

Steps to encourage positive thinking

- Create a safe place for young people to express and share negative feelings.

- Create feelings flash cards to encourage young people to build their emotional literacy and to identify their actual feelings, for example, 'I feel confused' rather than 'I'm mad'.

- Encourage 'possibility thinking', encouraging young people to play with suspending reality and considering alternative potentials. For example, 'What if you didn't feel that way? What if you thought the opposite was true? What thoughts would you think if you believed in yourself?'

- Keep a thoughts and feelings diary, or use the Thoughts and Feelings Graph in Part 3 to explore the correlation between thoughts, feelings and behaviours, helping young people to build self-awareness.

- Use affirmation techniques (the process of creating and repeating an affirmative statement to balance negative thinking). (Affirmation activities can be found in Part 3.)

- Find the roots of negative thoughts – do the thoughts actually belong to someone else? Some patterns of thinking become adopted when we hear them often, such as the child who is bullied and constantly hears 'you're fat and ugly'. Eventually the child owns this thought. Help young people to identify whose voice the negative thoughts sound like and disassociate from it.

- Take the positive from negative thoughts. Instead of 'I failed the test, so I'm stupid' the thought becomes 'I failed the test, so I need to dedicate more time to studying in the future.'

- Get in touch with positive feelings and explore their root in positive thoughts. Help young people to explore the physical presence of good feelings and identify where in their body they experience happiness, confidence, joy, and so forth. Use imagery to help anchor the feeling, such as visualizing the feeling as a certain colour or shape. (This is explored further in activities in Part 3.)

- Change the negative state using NLP (see Chapter 11).

- Test the validity of thoughts – how realistic are they? Use the challenging core beliefs activities, such as Activity 1.12: Beliefs and Activity 1.13: Challenging Limiting Beliefs.

- Place negative thoughts on a continuum, from negative to positive. As encouraging children to reverse a pervasive negative thought can be too much of a leap, however, find the middle ground initially, until the child is able to progress further. For example, original thought: 'I am a terrible person.' Positive thought: 'I am a wonderful person.' Middle ground: 'I am an okay person.'

Automatic negative thoughts

Automatic negative thoughts can be described as thoughts or images that pop into our mind, often bypassing our conscious attention and leaving us with a negative emotion or state. These can be based upon our core limiting beliefs and are often habitual and persistent. They often seem like fact and totally believable, and can therefore be difficult to identify and to challenge.

Automatic thoughts can be triggered in stressful or traumatic situations, by particular people, or by situations that key into our limiting beliefs. Each time a similar situation occurs, the negative thought automatically comes to mind, seeming like fact. Automatic negative thoughts can fall into the following categories:

- *Black and white thinking:* 'I failed my science test again. School is so pointless.'

- *Over-generalization:* 'I never get things right.'

- *Filtering out the positives and focusing on the negatives:* 'The whole dance performance was perfect apart from the last minute. I know I won't win now and everyone will laugh at me.'

- *Mind reading:* 'That was such a dumb joke I told. I bet she thinks I'm a total loser now.'

- *Personalization:* 'Sarah didn't text me back. She doesn't want to be my friend any more, I just know it.'

- *Disaster thinking:* 'If I don't lose weight I'll never get a boyfriend.'

- *Fortune telling thinking:* 'He definitely won't want to go out on a date with me again. He thought I was boring. There's no point in trying to contact him again.'

Figure 10.1 highlights the process of automatic negative thoughts taking root, and their impact on a person's behaviour.

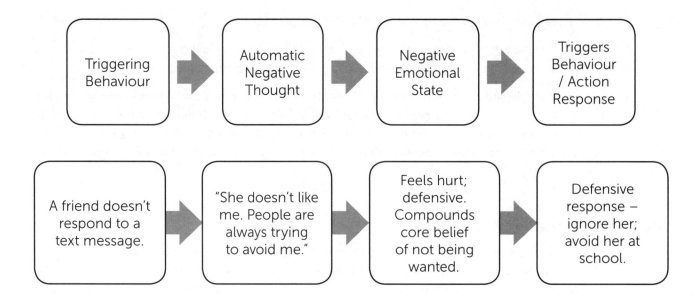

Figure 10.1: The Process of Automatic Negative Thoughts

Challenging automatic negative thoughts

The process for challenging and reframing negative and unhelpful automatic thoughts is similar to the process for challenging limiting beliefs; negative thoughts are often based upon limiting beliefs. The key to reframing thoughts into a neutral or positive state is awareness. Without being aware of the presence of negative thoughts, and aware of the impact of those thoughts on our feelings and behaviour, we are powerless to create change.

Challenging negative automatic thoughts with children and young people requires a simple, step-by-step process that is easy to understand and follow. A worksheet for identifying and challenging negative thoughts is found in Part 3 (Worksheet 16), encompassing the following steps:

1. Become aware of the thought: 'What am I thinking right now? What was I thinking to feel that way? What went through my head at that moment?'

2. Challenge the thought: 'Is it true? How do I know? Does this thought make me feel good or bad? Is this thought 100 per cent fact?'

3. Find the evidence for and against: 'How would I know this thought was true? How would I know this thought wasn't true?'

4. Identify a more helpful thought: 'What could I think instead that would make me feel better? What are some other thoughts I could think instead?'

Self-talk

Self-talk is a useful concept to explore with children and young people. The internal voice that speaks to us, often without our conscious awareness, can be a constant positive or negative force, shaping our feelings and experience of the world. The internal voice often chatters away without limit – controlling and shaping our self-talk is a powerful way to create a better frame of mind and emotional state.

As with negative automatic thoughts and limiting beliefs, becoming aware of our internal chatter is the first step. Encourage young people to identify the different types of chatter that go through their mind to pinpoint negative examples. Our self-talk might chatter away about innocuous themes such as what we're going to have for dinner, or what we're going to do when we get home tonight. Or when a child looks in the mirror her self-talk might turn ugly, filling her mind with hateful and mean-spirited thoughts, focusing on the aspects of her features she dislikes the most.

The quality of a young person's self-talk might depend on her frame of mind at any given time. On a good day looking in the mirror reflects positive self-talk: 'My hair looks good today.' A bad day can evoke the opposite response. This is a natural part of life – from time to time life will get us down. This type of self-talk isn't overly concerning if it is balanced by a mostly positive internal voice, or the young person can challenge her internal voice. For example, 'I hate my hair today. What a mess I look. But at least my skin looks clear and bright.'

Persistently negative self-talk that is linked to negative automatic thoughts is more concerning. Sometimes this constant, critical companion is actually an echo of someone else's voice. It may sound just like a critical parent or teacher, repeating the same words and phrases we heard from a key figure in our life. Asking questions about the 'voice' can help young people to identify whether it is a reflection of their thoughts, or someone else's, and can therefore help to challenge whether their self-talk is fact.

Techniques to reframe self-talk

- Acknowledge the thought and reframe it into something more positive: 'I am so fat and ugly' can become 'I feel as though I am overweight and am taking steps to become healthier.'

- Personalize self-talk: explore how the voice sounds in the child's mind and change it into less critical, harmless chatter by changing the tone of the voice, lowering its volume, and making it sound playful. For example, encourage the child to try and make it squeaky and high pitched or deep and gravelly – imagine it as the voice of a harmless, fluffy little puppy!

- Create your own internal voice: explore what someone who cared deeply for the child would sound like. What would she say? How would her voice sound?

- Practise responses to self-talk for specific situations that a young person identifies as troublesome, for example, looking in the mirror. Create a list that she can keep to hand if needed.

- Use affirmations: 'I am a good person' or 'I am perfect just the way I am.'

The saboteur

The critical internal voice or mean-spirited self-talk is sometimes described as the 'saboteur'. This judgemental voice can lead people to self-sabotage – destroying their progress towards goals and positive feelings. The saboteur can be a powerful voice and one that holds much sway. It is the voice that says, 'There's no point in trying, you'll only fail again' or 'Remember what happened last time – you don't want to put yourself out there to get hurt again.' The saboteur's cautious voice often lurks unnoticed and may sound like a positive influence, acting to keep a person safe and avoid risks. However, the saboteur can link to limiting beliefs, replaying a negative record of fear and judgement. The saboteur is often awoken by change – taking steps to make big changes in our life can spark the internal voice that warns of impending disaster or failure, stopping people in their tracks. An activity to explore the inner critic's voice can be found in Part 3 (Worksheet 21).

Relaxation techniques

Exploring and challenging negative thoughts and feelings can be highly effective, and helps to build children's social and emotional intelligence, as well as self-awareness. For some young people the connection between mind and body is strong, and their negative thoughts and limiting beliefs impact upon their physical health and body. Persistently negative thoughts can create anxiety and depression, causing a whole host of physical complaints, including tension in the body, headaches, stomach and digestive complaints, somatic problems, skin conditions and so forth.

Focusing on thoughts and feelings is one part of the good health puzzle, but some children will respond more readily to action-based activities that connect mind and body. Helping children to relax and de-stress builds lifelong skills to be used on a daily basis or when stressful events occur, such as sitting exams or learning to drive.

Relaxation techniques include:

- breathing exercises

- meditation

- visualization

- exercise

- stretching

- mindfulness.

A selection of visualization scripts are included in Part 3 of *Life Coaching for Kids*, and can be adapted to use in a variety of situations. There are various ways to relax and re-centre, but often we associate relaxing with participating in an activity where our body is still but our mind is active, such as watching TV or reading a book. While these are perfectly acceptable forms of relaxation it is important to provide young people with methods to turn off their mind as well as body. Unplugging computers and TVs, turning off phones and focusing on the physical state provides a deeper sense of relaxation. This is particularly important for very introspective young people and those with a generally negative mind frame. Breathing, stretching and calming techniques are included in Part 3 and can be modelled and taught to young people.

Chapter summary

- Our mind and body are interconnected – good physical health impacts upon mental health and vice versa.

- The quality of our thoughts determines the quality of our lives – helping young people to develop positive thinking is important.

- Automatic negative thoughts are 'pop-up' thoughts bypassing our conscious attention and leaving us with a negative emotion or state.

- Self-talk can echo negative thoughts and limiting beliefs.

- Relaxation techniques connect mind and body and help to manage stress.

Chapter 11

Cognitive Behavioural Therapy and Neuro-Linguistic Programming

Cognitive behavioural therapy (CBT) and neuro-linguistic programming (NLP) are two approaches that complement life coaching well. The theories and tools of both CBT and NLP are often used in coaching to help shift a person's patterns of thinking and to create rapid changes in behaviour. Therapists train for many years in these approaches to fully grasp the underpinning theories and master the more complex strategies of CBT and NLP. Therefore using these techniques within life coaching should be attempted with care and an appreciation of the limits of proficiency. The CBT and NLP techniques included in *Life Coaching for Kids* are deliberately simple and based upon basic theory. If a child responds well to either approach you may wish to refer him to a trained and qualified cognitive behavioural therapist in his area, or NLP practitioner who can assist beyond surface-level intervention.

Cognitive behavioural therapy

CBT is derived from cognitive therapy, developed in the 1960s by Dr Aaron T. Beck, an American psychiatrist. It is a very practical, skills-based approach that explores the link between a person's thoughts and behaviour. CBT theorizes that our perceptions and thoughts influence our feelings, which in turn create a behaviour response. By changing our patterns of thinking we create a better emotional state, and react in a more positive way.

For example, if our thoughts are focused around getting something wrong or failing, we may likely feel stressed, anxious and nervous. This in turn can create a physiological response – our body reacts to this heightened level of stress and anxiety, pumping out adrenalin which leads us to splutter over our words, muddle our thinking, or forget our carefully rehearsed lines. Thus, our thoughts have created a negative behaviour response. In another sense our thoughts can affect our future behaviour. We think about failing, feel nervous, distressed and fearful, and avoid trying or give up altogether.

As explored earlier, our thoughts are not fact – they are merely stories we tell ourselves that often feel true. Patterns of thinking can be built upon ingrained negative and limiting beliefs that we are scarcely aware of, despite the havoc they cause in our day-to-day life.

CBT explores two main facets:

- *Cognition:* our thinking processes and perception.

- *Behaviour:* how we react and behave.

CBT strategies help people to identify unwanted patterns of thought, explore the impact of these thoughts upon their emotional state and behaviour, and create positive change in a goal-oriented process. By identifying more realistic and effective thoughts a person can lower his emotional distress and manage self-defeating behaviour. By acquiring and consolidating skills to retrain his thought processes and reactions, the person is in control of current and future problems. CBT is therefore a solution-focused and action-oriented approach, much the same as life coaching. Indeed, life coaching could be described as a form or extension of CBT.

Given that CBT is a very practical approach it is often well-suited to children and young people who are familiar with a skills-based learning process. CBT also helps young people to understand the roots of their behaviour, which can often feel reactive and automatic, out of their control. Many children won't have the cognitive reasoning or verbal ability to communicate why they fly off the handle in the classroom, or argue with their parents. They often don't know how to stop this behaviour, because they don't know why they do it in the first place. CBT helps children to explore the triggers for their behaviours in their thought processes, and understand how their feelings create a reaction, helping to build self-awareness and emotional literacy.

In this way CBT separates the behaviour from the person: rather than labelling a child as being a 'bad boy' for getting aggressive at school, instead the behaviour is labelled as the problem – being aggressive is bad. This avoids children becoming labelled and stigmatized and self-fulfilling prophecies from taking root as the child begins to own the label of being bad, for example, and embrace it with further inappropriate behaviour.

For CBT to be truly effective it requires a certain level of motivation. Practice and effort are required to challenge automatic negative thoughts, ingrained patterns of thinking and limiting beliefs, and to embed new ways of thinking. Nobody will be able to reflect upon and challenge every single thought they have – this would likely drive them crazy! But to become aware of situations that trigger negative thought and to invoke the skills learned will require effort and determination. Homework exercises and journaling can be a useful way to encourage people to embrace their learning.

Activities using the principles of CBT with children and young people can be found in Part 3. These help young people to identify the link between their thoughts, feelings and behaviours; manage anxiety; differentiate fact from feeling; and learn new ways of behaving to produce better results.

Neuro-linguistic programming

NLP is the study of subjective experience. Like CBT the focus is on a person's thoughts and actions. In essence, NLP is a method of personal development, a model of effective communication and a means of creating new behaviours.

The term 'neuro-linguistic programming' refers to the three themes of the approach:

- *Neuro:* focusing on the neurological (or thought) processes of a person.

- *Linguistic:* examining the language structures of a person.

- *Programming:* exploring the behavioural patterns and actions learned by experience.

NLP theory asserts that there is a connection between our thoughts, language, actions and learned patterns of behaviour that can be changed (often using rapid techniques) to achieve a specific goal or outcome. NLP was devised by Richard Bandler and John Grinder in the 1970s, as a result of the study of excellence in people. Bandler and Grinder developed methods to reproduce the techniques used by successful people and experts, so others could achieve similar results. Today there are many different applications of NLP, including within therapeutic settings, business and sales strategies, and sports coaching. When coaching children and young people, the use of NLP relates to relaxation, inducing creative visualization, and exploring the dynamic between the child's mind, language and processing or behaviour, on a fairly surface level. Some NLP techniques are simple and practical, and therefore well-suited for use with children and young people. Other NLP techniques are more complex and require a coach to undergo further training to ensure they are working effectively and ethically.

Key principles of NLP

SENSORY AWARENESS

NLP uses the senses to provide detail and to connect people to their thought processes and programming, to create new beliefs. The senses are: visual (what we see), auditory (what we hear), kinesthetic (touch and feel), olfactory (smell), and gustatory (taste). In NLP the senses are referred to as 'modalities'. 'Submodalities' are another level of our senses with finer detail, for example, a picture we visualize is in full colour or black and white; bright and clear, or fuzzy around the edges. These added bits of information – submodalities – are 'building blocks' to code our memory of sensory experience. They help to tell our brain whether something is important or not. Using the senses and submodalities in NLP helps to change a person's attachment and emotional response to a thought or memory. For example, when a child thinks of a person bullying him the image in his mind is strong and bright, which feels very real and therefore frightening. The child remembers his bullying experience vividly each time the image is recalled. NLP techniques can help to change that image so that it has less of an effect upon the child, thus altering his emotional state.

Some children lean towards a visual learning style, while others are more auditory focused and need to hear information to process it. Some children need to experience learning by doing. Keying in to children's natural learning styles can make NLP techniques more effective.

OUTCOME THINKING

In NLP, as with coaching in general, the focus is on the outcome the person wishes to create. It is goal and action-oriented, helping people to shift their perception from their current position to considering possible future outcomes.

BEHAVIOURAL FLEXIBILITY

NLP techniques help people to become more flexible in their thinking and behaviour, to get better results.

SEPARATING THE BEHAVIOUR FROM THE PERSON

As with CBT, NLP asserts that the person is not his behaviour, that is, there is a distinction between the person and his actions – just because he has behaved badly doesn't necessarily make him a bad person. This helps to avoid people labelling themselves or confusing their behaviour with their identity.

This is particularly important for children and young people, who can quickly label themselves or gain negative labels from peers or key adult figures which stick for life. Consider the child who is the class clown, the 'nerd' or 'geek', the class bully, or school bad boy. The behaviours become part of the person's identity, until they are one and the same – 'I am a troublemaker.'

THE MAP IS NOT THE TERRITORY

This key concept of NLP describes the difference between a person's perception and reality. The 'map' refers to the perceptions we have, based upon our thoughts, beliefs, values, memories and experiences. The 'territory' refers to reality. Sometimes the two can be at cross-purposes as a person confuses his perception for truth and reality.

Each person's 'map' will be different, with our own experiences and perceptions of the world. When our reality is not working out as we would like, or we are struggling to make positive changes, NLP techniques can help us to explore and rewrite our 'map'.

NLP comprises of a number of techniques to change people's thoughts and patterns of behaviour. The NLP technique of resource anchoring is explored below, with further activities based on NLP techniques included in Part 3.

Resource anchoring

Resource anchoring is an NLP tool to help people manage their emotional state. Anchoring is used to associate and 'anchor' a positive thought to an event or situation, using memory, emotion and a trigger. For example, for a person with a tremendous fear of flying, the thoughts of disaster, dying and being out of control when flying become replaced with a neutral reaction, or flying even becomes fun!

The process of anchoring is used to help people disassociate negative thoughts and feelings with a particular event, person, or situation, and instead replace the association with a positive emotional state that the person is in control of. Through this process the person can create a natural association with the positive state, calling upon the feeling at will. Anchoring is designed to link the new, positive response with the original event to such a degree that in time, the person will have created a whole new, natural, response to something he previously feared or avoided.

The process of using resource anchoring is as follows:

1. identifying the problem scenario

2. defining positive emotions to attach to the scenario (resources)

3. exploring memories of a time when the person felt those positive emotions

4. triggering those memories at will

5. creating a relaxed state

6. recalling the positive memories and associating it with a future state, related to the problem scenario (anchoring); this is often a simple physical action, such as touching thumb and middle finger together, or using a word as an anchor that can be repeated again.

The list above is a simplified version of a process that may take some time to complete. Skilled NLP practitioners will encourage people to add as much detail as possible to their positive memories, using the senses to create a richer experience. They may also encourage people to use their submodalities (finer details of their senses) to create an even stronger connection to the positive memory, such as listening for sounds or words as they recall the memory; creating a brighter and more vivid visual image; noticing how the body feels and connecting with tactile and emotional sensations; and recalling any smells or tastes related to the positive thought.

By repeating this process and adding greater detail to the positive state, the person creates a stronger depth of feeling and a more genuine experience. This positive state can then be called upon at will and experienced in the here-and-now.

The following example explores using resource anchoring with an unconfident child. (A script for using this process with a child or young person can be found in Activity 5.4: Confidence Visualization.) The process is deliberately simplified for use with children, but can be tailored to address a range of unresourceful states and problematic scenarios.

1. **Identifying the problem scenario:** a young woman is experiencing a lack of confidence, particularly related to her self-image. She feels ugly and disheartened when she looks in the mirror. She does not feel confident when she is with others and is becoming more of a recluse, wanting to stay at home where people can't see her.

2. **Defining positive emotions to attach to the scenario (resources):** she identifies the positive state of being truly confident, feeling secure, being proud of the way she looks and happy within herself.

3. **Exploring memories of a time when the person felt those positive emotions:** she identifies a time when she felt secure and confident, when she was spending time with her best friend before the other girl moved away. She remembers dressing up to go to a party with her friend and feeling good when she looked in the mirror.

4. **Triggering those memories at will:** the coach encourages her to visualize seeing herself in the mirror as the most confident and positive version of herself. The coach describes her reflection in detail, for example, her skin is glowing and her eyes are bright. The light is reflecting from her shiny hair. Her smile is wide and infectious. Her body feels relaxed and yet strong. She can feel that her head is held high, her back is straight and her shoulders relaxed. She can smell the fragrance of a light, flowery perfume she is wearing, and feel the soft cotton of the dress against her smooth skin. As she looks in the mirror she can hear her best friend telling her how good she looks.

   The coach and the young woman may need to repeat this process a number of times to fully engage with the positive state. Adding new detail can help, and the coach can also encourage the young woman to make the image of herself in the mirror bigger in her mind's eye, brighter, clearer, and so forth. Or she might imagine she is watching a video of herself looking confident, relaxed and pretty. When she is ready she can make the TV screen much bigger and 'step into' the video in her mind's eye, embodying the new version of herself.

5. **Creating a relaxed state:** the coach and young woman focus on her breathing, helping her to find a relaxed state. The coach may encourage her to feel her muscles relaxing, and to let go of any anxiety in her body and mind.

6. **Recalling the positive memories and associating it with a future state, related to the problem scenario (anchoring):** the coach and young woman recall the positive state once more. The young woman visualizes herself in front of the mirror and repeats the process above. She identifies the peak moment within the scene where she feels the most confident and at ease and at that moment triggers an anchor. She presses together her thumb and middle finger on her left hand and repeats the word 'confident' to herself.

   The coach and young woman repeat this process a number of times to ensure that the positive state is truly anchored and she can call upon this new state at will. They explore her presenting concern and identify whether her perception of the original scenario has shifted at all. The young woman might want to try the anchoring process in different scenarios and practise using it. She may want to then develop additional anchors for associated scenarios, such as feeling confident in the classroom, or when making new friends.

Resource anchoring may not be suitable for every child or young person, and coaches will need to use their judgement before using NLP techniques.

The activities included in *Life Coaching for Kids* provide very simplified versions of CBT and NLP techniques that are safe to use with children and easy to understand. Those wanting to know more about these two approaches may benefit from further study.

Chapter summary

- Cognitive behavioural therapy (CBT) and neuro-linguistic programming (NLP) are two approaches that complement life coaching well.

- CBT is a practical, skills-based approach that explores the link between a person's thoughts and behaviour, theorizing that our perceptions and thoughts influence our feelings, which in turn create a behaviour response.

- NLP is a method of personal development, a model of effective communication and a means of creating new behaviours.

- NLP focuses on the neurological (or thought) processes of people, their language structures and 'programming' – the behavioural patterns and actions learned by experience.

Part 3

Life Coaching for Kids Activities

Chapter 12

Activities and Worksheets

The *Life Coaching for Kids* activities and worksheets are designed to be flexible in approach, and most can be used for a variety of youth issues or situations. Coaches are encouraged to be creative with the activities to ensure they meet the needs of individual children.

Hints and tips

- Coaches may wish to use a 'pick and mix' approach to using the activities, selecting those best suited to the young person being supported, or work in a consecutive manner through the activities.

- Use the activities as a starting point for discussion, to learn more about the young people and develop their self-awareness.

- Keep coaching fresh by interspersing activities with games, turning resources into creative arts activities, and so forth.

- Give young people copies of worksheets and activities to do at home, or to use post-coaching to remember their responses and learning.

- Use the activities in different ways – for example, use the General Scaling Tool to measure the effects of bullying, or use a confidence activity to help a young person with self-image concerns.

- When using a visualization script, ensure the young person is willing to participate. Create a safe, quiet place to conduct the visualization, and ensure that you read the script slowly, with a soft and gentle tone of voice. Encourage the young person to close her eyes and relax, but stress that she can open her eyes and stop at any time. This is not a hypnosis or state-changing exercise in any way; it is simply the process of focusing the mind on a positive thought. You can add detail and specific information into a visualization to meet the needs of a child, for example, centring a visualization around a football field if this is a place you know the child feels safe and happy.

You may wish to start the coaching process by using one of the initial activities such as the Wheel of Life or General Scaling Tool. When you have learned more about why the child has come for coaching support you can use the Life Coaching Action Plan to make a weekly or sessional plan, and/or use the weekly progress sheet to keep track. Remember above all to keep coaching positive – reflect on the child's progress and acknowledge her successes regularly.

For those using the coaching tools in a formal or structured setting, a feedback sheet for each young person to complete on completion of coaching can be found in Worksheet 42. This can help to measure the success of coaching and gain feedback to improve the service provided.

Theme 1
General Activities

Activity 1.1: Starting Coaching

Resources required	*Worksheet 1: Checklist for Coaching; Worksheet 2: Coaching Appointment Reminder Cards; Worksheet 3: Life Coaching Action Plan; Worksheet 4: Weekly Progress Sheet*
Activity aims	*To prepare for coaching sessions*

Before embarking on a coaching session, review Worksheet 1: Checklist for Coaching to ensure you are ready and equipped to coach. This is not an exhaustive list and can change depending on the setting or way in which you are using the coaching materials. You may also wish to make copies of the following resources:

- Worksheet 2: Coaching Appointment Reminder Cards.

- Worksheet 3: Life Coaching Action Plan.

- Worksheet 4: Weekly Progress Sheet.

Appointment cards can be given to young people attending regular coaching sessions, to help them and/or their parents remember the dates and times of future sessions. You may wish to print these on thin card.

Worksheet 3 contains an action plan for you to track each individual young person's progress through coaching. This plan is for the coach and can be completed after the young person has left the session. The plan can be used to detail the focus of the time spent and add notes to remind yourself of any follow-up activities or actions you need to make, such as exploring the theme of bullying in the next session, or making a referral for family therapy.

Finally, Worksheet 4, the Weekly Progress Sheet, can be taken home and used by the young person to keep track of her goals and actions between sessions. This resource is typically better suited to older young people and those who are self-directed and wish to make notes as they go through the coaching process.

It is recommended for coaches to provide a journal or notebook for each young person to keep and take home, depending on their age. This journal can be used to record thoughts, feelings, goals, affirmations, homework activities and so on. They can bring the journal to each session to discuss their entries with their coach, or keep it as a private resource.

Activity 1.2: Wheel of Life

Resources required	*Worksheet 5: Wheel of Life*
Activity aims	*To identify the focus of coaching*
	To explore the different aspects of life that may be out of balance

The Wheel of Life helps young people to identify which parts of their life might be out of balance or in need of attention. This activity can be used to help clarify the goals and focus of coaching, to bring positive reflection by establishing the parts of a young person's life that are working well, or to create a long-term strategy for coaching.

Using Worksheet 5: Wheel of Life, explore each segment of the wheel with the young person, discussing which parts of her life might fall within each category. For example, 'Home' might include the young person's relationship with parents and siblings, living environment, etc.

The young person should rate each part of her life on a scale of 1–10, with '1' being very poor/extremely dissatisfactory, and '10' indicating very good/entirely satisfactory. She should mark her score on the line, on each part of the wheel. When ready, join together the marks around the wheel.

In an ideal situation the Wheel of Life would represent a perfect circle, with each part of the young person's life being a '10' and in perfect balance. Discuss any low-scoring elements, assisting the young person to reflect upon which elements in that part of her life are most in need of change. This can then form the basis of a goal setting action plan.

If a number of aspects of the young person's life are low scoring, prioritize which themes to focus on initially. Balance this discussion by reflecting upon the positives in her life, too.

Activity 1.3: Connecting With Feelings

Resources required	*Worksheet 6: Connecting With Feelings; pens; small strips of coloured card; glue; paper*
Activity aims	*To build emotional vocabulary and connect young people to their feelings*
	To assist young people to connect with their positive emotions

Ask the young person to identify some words to describe her feelings on a good and bad day. Encourage deeper exploration beyond 'happy', 'sad', or 'angry' by exploring different scenarios, such as, 'How would you feel if...':

- You were being bullied?

- You got an 'A' on a test at school?

- You had to move to a new school where you didn't know anybody?

- You had a big argument with your parents?

- You found a lot of money and could keep it?

- You were asked to spend the day with someone you really like being with?

Ask the young person to write each feeling word on a strip of coloured card, with one feeling per card. When a good selection of both positive and negative words have been identified, ask the young person to place them in order from the best feeling to the worst, in a ladder shape. Stress that there are no right or wrong answers, just her opinion. Glue each strip to a large sheet of paper, to keep and refer back to during subsequent sessions.

When complete, explore Worksheet 6: Connecting with Feelings. This should help the young person to connect with her positive feelings, and identify a time when she felt those emotions. This can be used to help focus the young person on her ultimate goal for coaching (to feel positively about themselves and their life), and can be used later in coaching during visualization or resource anchoring activities, such as Activity 2.5: Forgiveness, Activity 3.3: Mind Movies, Activity 4.2: The Shield and Activity 5.4: Confidence Visualization.

Activity 1.4: My Priorities

Resources required	*Worksheet 7: My Priorities; pens; coloured markers*
Activity aims	*To build rapport with a young person and strengthen the coaching relationship*
	To learn more about the young person and develop awareness about her needs and life issues
	To encourage the young person to set her priorities and begin to explore goal setting in coaching

This activity can help to build an initial relationship with young people, gathering information about their interests and passions, and potential issues of concern, in a non-threatening manner. This activity can also be repeated at the end of the coaching relationship, as a measurement tool, to explore whether the young person's self-perception has changed over the course of coaching.

Explore Worksheet 7: My Priorities, completing each box together. The young person can add words, phrases or images within each of the categories, depending on her age and ability level. Encourage her to reflect upon each element in turn, asking questions to prompt further response if needed

At this stage of the coaching relationship the focus should be on information gathering, relationship building and helping the young person to feel at ease. Generate discussion about the young person's hobbies, interests, likes and dislikes, and experience of life, offering your own reflections if appropriate. If a child cannot identify anything to write or draw within a particular category, prompt her thinking with open questions, such as:

- If you had a whole day to do whatever you liked, what would you do?

- If someone gave you a lot of money, how would you spend it?

- How would your friends describe you?

- What words might your parents or guardians use to describe you?

This activity should provide an indication of where the young person is struggling, or where problems are occurring.

Activity 1.5: Values

Resources required	*Worksheet 8: Things That Are Important to Me; Worksheet 9: Values List*
Activity aims	*To identify life values* *To explore where values are not being met in life* *To begin to identify goals in coaching*

Explore Worksheet 8: Things That Are Important to Me. Encourage the young person to write down as many things she can think of that describe the parts of life that are most important to her. This might include people, activities, hobbies, tangible things, or values words (for example, 'independence').

When complete, review the list of values in Worksheet 9. Explore any words the young person doesn't understand or is unsure of. Ask the young person to circle any words that she feels are important to her in life, such as being in control or feeling adventurous. Make a list of her top five values and discuss whether these values are being met in her life currently, or not.

Place the two worksheets side by side and review the young person's list of things that are important to her, against her values. Explore the values that each of those important things represent, for example, the young person identifies going shopping with friends as something important to her. This might represent the value of friendship, freedom or beauty. Write a value word to represent each important part of her life that she has listed. Explore how those values are currently being met in her life, or might be missing. Refer back to this list of values when goal setting, to ensure that the young person's goals are aligned with her values.

Note: This activity is most appropriate for older young people, who can understand the concept of life values.

Activity 1.6: General Scaling

Resources required   *Worksheet 10: General Scaling Tool*

Activity aims   *To identify the young person's current level of well-being*
To project a future level of well-being as a focus for coaching
To measure progress towards goals and track improvements

The General Scaling Tool can be used to measure general well-being, or to measure a young person's perception of a specific issue, such as bullying. Scaling also helps to put problems into a realistic perspective, and can measure progress across a number of coaching sessions.

Using Worksheet 10, ask the young person to choose a number value to describe her life as a whole (or in relation to a specific issue, for example, a number to describe how much bullying is affecting her life), where '1' is very poor, and '10' is perfect. The young person should describe how she knows she is 'at' that number. List her responses on a separate piece of paper or on the back of the worksheet.

Now ask the young person to identify which number describes where she would like to get to in the future, circling it on the second scale. You may wish to choose a specific timeframe, such as by the end of coaching, the end of the school year, etc. Discuss and list how she would know if she was 'at' that number. Carefully encourage young people to be realistic in this process. Jumping from a '1' to a '10' in a matter of weeks may not happen, but a '2' to a '7' might be achievable. Discuss how the young person would know she was 'at' that higher number. What would be different in her life or within herself? List her responses.

Next, identify a small goal of moving one point along the scale, for example, from her starting point at a '2' to a '3'. Discuss how she could move one point along the scale. What could she do to make that small change? By focusing on small steps progress is manageable and more likely to occur. Repeat this progress within each coaching session, slowly moving up a point or two along the scale each session.

Record progress and triumphs and reflect on how far the young person has come, identifying the strategies she has used to make this happen.

Activity 1.7: Goal Setting

Resources required *Worksheet 11: Goal Setting Brainstorming; Worksheet 12: Goal Setting Action Plan*

Activity aims *To identify and set goals for coaching*
To create an action plan to reach the goal

Review Worksheet 11: Goal Setting Brainstorming, and support the young person to complete each section of the brainstorm on the worksheet, or to draw it out on a larger sheet of paper she can refer back to. When coaching groups you may wish to complete the brainstorming exercise together on a large sheet of paper, and then encourage young people to work individually to complete Worksheet 12: Goal Setting Action Plan.

Referring back to the completed brainstorm (and other information gathered from using the Wheel of Life exercise, General Scaling Tool, or general discussions), set a short, medium and long-term goal with the young person, completing Worksheet 12.

You may wish to prompt the young person to explore her goal by asking questions such as:

- If you could change one thing in your life that would make the most difference, what would it be?

- What would you like us to work on first?

- How could life be even better for you?

Remember to ensure goals are SMART (Specific, Measurable, Attainable, Realistic and Timely). If a young person's goal is too broad, help her to specify. For example, 'I want to go to university' might be refocused as 'I want to pass my upcoming secondary school exams.' Make a note of wider goals and discuss other smaller steps the young person could take to reach them.

Discuss the action plan and work together to set short-term 'markers' (smaller goals) and timeframes. The action plan can be referred and added to throughout the coaching sessions.

Activity 1.8: Making Decisions

Resources required	*Worksheet 13: Gains and Losses Worksheet*
Activity aims	*To explore the impact of decisions and choices*
	To build young people's self-awareness
	To improve behaviour and relationships with others

Discuss some of the ways in which we make decisions, for example, by thinking something through carefully and making a conscious choice, or by going with the crowd, following others, letting ourselves be led, etc. Discuss the consequences for the choices we make, and how we can become aware of what will happen before we make a decision.

Complete Worksheet 13: Gains and Losses. This can be used in conjunction with Worksheet 12: Goal Setting Action Plan, or discuss specific behaviours or choices the young person makes. When using the worksheet to explore a particular goal, encourage the young person to think about what might be some of the 'pay-offs' or reasons why she would not want to change, as well as some of the reasons why she *would* want to change. This can help the young person to identify whether she is ready to reach her goal or needs to identify an easier target. She can also refer back to this worksheet in the future when she is losing focus or getting off-track from her goal.

Explore the concept of 'gains' and 'losses'. If easier, the young person could consider the positives and the negatives of each decision. For example:

If I choose to...	Gains	Losses
Skip school	Popularity People think I'm cool	Fall behind in class Get into trouble Flunk out of school
Reach my goal of not bullying others	I feel better about myself People will like being with me I won't get into trouble	People might pick on me I won't be popular

Activity 1.9: Thoughts and Feelings

Resources required   *Worksheet 14: Thoughts and Feelings Graph*

Activity aims   *To explore the link between a young person's thoughts and feelings*
To build emotional literacy and awareness

This activity can be used to help young people:

- identify negative patterns of thinking

- explore the link between their thoughts and feelings

- identify triggers to negative thoughts and feelings

- avoid people, situations or patterns of thinking that create negative emotion.

Using Worksheet 14: Thoughts and Feelings Graph, explore the young person's thoughts and feelings of the previous day (or a recent day when a specific situation occurred). She should plot her feelings against the time axis, using the scale of 1–10, where '1' is feeling very bad, and '10' is feeling great.

Once the young person has plotted her feelings throughout the day she should pick a few 'high' or 'low' moments and write a few words to describe what her thoughts were at that time.

DISCUSS WITH THE YOUNG PERSON

- How do your thoughts influence your feelings?

- If you had to choose a number to describe your feelings generally, on a day-to-day basis, what would it be?

- Which thoughts could you change to create better feelings?

Activity 1.10: Thoughts, Feelings and Behaviours

Resources required   *Worksheet 15: Thoughts, Feelings, Behaviours*

Activity aims   *To explore the link between thoughts, feelings and behaviours*
To build self-awareness

This activity explores the link between a young person's thoughts, feelings and behaviours. By changing her thoughts, the young person can create a more positive emotional state, and different results.

Using the first part of the worksheet, explore a recent situation the young person is struggling with, or a general negative pattern of thought, and how it is affecting her. In the first box she should record her thoughts about the situation. Next she should record her feelings, and then what happens as a result of these thoughts and feelings, that is, her behaviours.

On the second part of the worksheet the young person should think of some alternative thoughts that could create better feelings and better behaviours or outcomes. This will require her to shift her mindset to explore other options and ways of seeing the situation, which can be challenging. You may need to encourage her with some suggestions and ideas. Finally, explore the new feelings and actions that would result from the new thoughts.

This activity should begin to help the young person reframe her perception about herself or problem situations, teaching her to get in the habit of challenging and questioning negative patterns of thought.

Activity 1.11: Automatic Thoughts

Resources required   *Worksheet 16: Automatic Thoughts*

Activity aims   *To understand and explore negative automatic thoughts*
To keep a record of automatic thoughts and begin to reframe them into positive thinking patterns

This activity helps a young person to identify and challenge negative automatic thoughts. By becoming more aware of her negative thoughts, the young person is better equipped to question and reframe her thinking.

Negative automatic thoughts are the thoughts that pop into the mind, often unconsciously, as a reaction to a situation, person, event, and so forth. They often tie in to limiting beliefs, and can create negative emotional states and cycles of negative thoughts.

Using Worksheet 16: Automatic Thoughts, encourage the young person to reflect upon or keep a record of any negative automatic thoughts she notices herself thinking. The young person should rate each thought from 1–100 depending on the degree to which the thought seems true, where '1' is completely untrue, and '100' is completely true. The young person should also record her feelings, where '1' is not feeling bad at all, and '100' is feeling extremely bad.

Finally, work with the young person to identify possible alternatives to these thoughts and explore what the results or outcome might be on her feelings and behaviours.

The young person can keep and add to her thought record between sessions, or may wish to keep track of any automatic thoughts she notices popping up, in her journal. This helps to build awareness of negative thought patterns.

Activity 1.12: Beliefs

Resources required	Worksheet 17: Belief Labels; scissors
Activity aims	To identify limiting core beliefs and the impact on the young person's life
	To begin to reframe negative beliefs

The belief labels found in Worksheet 17 can be used in a variety of activities and in response to a range of issues. These labels help the young person and coach to become aware of the limiting core beliefs the young person may hold, which are negatively impacting upon her life and well-being.

Copy and cut up the belief labels and place them face up across a table (you may wish to laminate them first so they are durable and long-lasting). Explain to the young person that each label is an example of a belief, something we believe is true about ourselves, others or the world in general. Some are positive; some are negative.

Ask the young person to select four or five labels that describe things she believes are true. She should choose the ones she most strongly believes, or that 'jump out' at her. Stress that there are no right or wrong answers.

When she is ready, read the chosen labels together and discuss. Explore the consequences of these beliefs, and how they impact upon the young person's life. Explore some of the ways the young person can challenge any negative beliefs.

Discuss with the young person

- Do any of these beliefs belong to someone else you know, that you have accepted as true?

- Might some of these negative beliefs be untrue?

- How do these beliefs make you feel? What impact do they have on your life?

- Choose a belief that you would like to be true. How can you change your thoughts so that you believed this to be true?

Note: The young person could choose one positive belief to focus on for the next week, exploring the belief in her journal.

Activity 1.13: Challenging Limiting Beliefs

Resources required	Worksheet 17: Belief Labels; scissors; Worksheet 18: Challenging Limiting Beliefs or Worksheet 19: Changing Beliefs
Activity aims	To understand the concept of negative core beliefs To identify the gains and costs of holding on to negative beliefs

This activity helps a young person to identify and challenge negative core beliefs. (More about core beliefs can be found in Chapter 9.)

You may become aware of a young person's negative and limiting core beliefs through the process of coaching, as the young person shares her thoughts and feelings. However, you may wish to use Worksheet 17: Belief Labels to help the young person identify her beliefs. Copy and cut up the labels, placing them across a table. Ask the young person to choose a selection of labels that describe things she believes in, as per the previous activity (Activity 1.12: Beliefs).

Discuss the impact of these beliefs. Are there any ways these beliefs cause the young person pain, or hold her back? Share with the young person the idea that sometimes there are reasons why we hold on to negative thoughts or beliefs. Even though they might cause us pain, they also give us something – a 'pay-off' – which might keep us stuck and unable to change our thoughts.

Explore Worksheet 18: Challenging Limiting Beliefs and if necessary, discuss each column and the example, to ensure the young person understands the concepts of a 'pay-off' and 'cost' for believing something. The young person might wish to record an example of a new, empowering belief in her journal.

An alternative to this exercise can be found in Worksheet 19 Changing Beliefs, whereby the young person grades her current limiting belief with a percentage rating, and explores the evidence to disprove the belief, helping to reframe her thoughts more positively. This may be an easier concept for younger children to understand than the activity above.

Activity 1.14: Mood and Thought Diary

Resources required   *Worksheet 20: Mood and Thought Record*

Activity aims   *To explore the link between thoughts and emotional state*

The Mood and Thought Record can be used on an ongoing basis or in response to a specific problem or emotional state.

The young person should record her feelings in the first box on Worksheet 20. Using a number from 1–10 can help young people who struggle with verbalizing their feelings, where '1' is not feeling bad at all, and '10' is feeling extremely bad.

Next the young person should record her thoughts and what's going through her mind, rating the helpfulness of the thoughts, where '1' is really helpful, and '10' is not helpful at all. Finally, the young person can identify whether anything happened to trigger these thoughts and feelings, such as something someone said, an incident, and so on.

This could lead to a discussion about negative automatic thoughts and changing thoughts to create better feelings. Relaxation techniques can also be used to help the young person to change her emotional state.

The Mood and Thought Record can be continued over the period of a few weeks or months to record any changes or developments in the young person's thinking and emotional state.

Activity 1.15: The Inner Critic

Resources required	*Worksheet 21: The Inner Critic*
Activity aims	*To understand and identify the 'inner critic' or 'saboteur'*
	To understand the impact of negative self-talk
	To reframe critical self-talk into a positive inner voice

Worksheet 21 introduces the concept of the 'inner critic'. You may wish to spend some time discussing and exploring the idea of self-talk and a person's inner voice, exploring whether the young person's inner voice is usually positive and helpful, or negative and critical.

Discuss how the inner critic sounds, and the sort of things the critic says, recording them on the worksheet. You may wish to explore whether the critic sounds like someone the young person knows, like a teacher or parent.

Discuss what happens to the young person when she hears her inner critic. How does she react? What happens next? Introduce the idea of having power and control over the inner critic, and encourage the young person to create a balance to the critic, recording it on the worksheet.

EXTENSION ACTIVITY

- Ask the young person to get into a comfortable position and practise some breathing techniques to relax.

- Ask her to imagine she can hear her inner critic now. She may wish to reflect on some of the ideas she wrote on the worksheet for what the critic might be saying.

- Now, ask her to imagine she's got a big remote control in her hand and can turn down the volume of the critic's voice. Ask her to do that now, in her mind's eye, until she can barely hear the critic anymore.

- Ask her to turn the volume up a little bit more, and to press a different button on the remote control. This one makes the inner critic sound squeaky and silly! She can press different buttons to play around with the critic's voice in her mind, until the voice loses some of its power. She can even press fast-forward or pause when she hears the inner critic start talking.

- Next, ask her to imagine she can hear the opposite of the critic, saying nice, supportive things. Again, you may wish to remind her of some of the things she wrote on the worksheet.

- Ask her to use the remote control in her mind's eye to turn the volume up louder.

- Reflect upon how it feels to hear such positive, supportive comments, leaving the young person in this frame of mind.

The young person can repeat this process at any time, whenever her self-talk becomes negative and unhelpful. This activity can also be extended to include creative activities to draw or create images of the inner critic and the opposite to the critic. The young person may wish to give names to her positive and negative self-talk, and use painting, sculpture, collage or creative writing to visualize the positive, supportive element within.

Activity 1.16: Daily Habits

Resources required   *Worksheet 22: Daily Habits*

Activity aims   *To identify negative habits of thinking and behaviours*
To explore the impact of positive and negative habits
To identify new habits of thinking and behaviours that would serve the young person well

This activity can be used to identify negative habits of thought and behaviours that can become problematic for young people.

Using Worksheet 22: Daily Habits, explore some examples of positive and negative habits. Initially it will be easier to focus on obvious positive habits of behaviour, such as brushing teeth or going to school. You may need to encourage the young person to explore her behaviour on a deeper level to become aware of negative habits, which can be quite entrenched, for example, not listening in science class, swearing and using bad language, or thinking that she has to tell jokes and be the class clown.

Explore the roots of these negative habits, recording the results on a separate sheet of paper. What leads the young person to misbehave in a certain teacher's class, or leave her bedroom untidy at home? This exercise can also link to thoughts, feelings and behaviour activities.

Explore and discuss the impact of the young person's positive habits. What are the consequences for these habits? Identify some of the characteristics and strengths the young person displays to engage in these positive habits. You may also wish to record these on a separate sheet of paper, to refer back to at a later date.

Activity 1.17: The Magic Question

Resources required	*Worksheet 23: The Magic Question*
Activity aims	*To explore the young person's frame of reference and mindset*
	To assist with goal setting and creating positive change
	To explore new ways of thinking and encourage new perceptions

The Magic or 'Miracle' Question helps to challenge a person's frame of mind, and open up her thinking to new possibilities.

Using Worksheet 23, ask the young person to consider: 'Imagine you went to bed one night and a miracle happened. How would you know? What would be different?'

Try and encourage the young person to not get too focused on what the actual miracle was or how it came about. Instead, focus the young person on the changes that occurred as a result of the miracle. Depending on the age and ability level of the young person, encourage her to consider what might be different inside her, as well as on the outside. For example:

- Would they see the world differently?

- Would they feel differently?

- How would people treat them now?

- What would have changed?

- What would have stayed the same?

Spend some time unpicking her 'miracle', exploring how she could make her miracle a reality, linking to her Goal Setting Action Plan. The young person can write or draw her responses on Worksheet 23 to refer back to at a later date.

For older young people you can extend this activity by asking the following question:

Imagine you woke up and a miracle had happened. Something inside of you had changed. Suddenly, you didn't believe a negative thought that you used to think anymore. How would you know? What would be different?

Activity 1.18: Powerful Questions

Resources required *Worksheet 24: Powerful Questions*

Activity aims *To build a relationship between a coach and young person*
To explore a young person's frame of reference and patterns of thinking
To assist with goal setting

Worksheet 24 contains some examples of powerful questions – questions to encourage young people to explore, debate, share their perspective and encourage new ways of thinking.

- If you could wave a magic wand, what would you change about your life?

- What is the best thing about being you?

- If you could have a super power, what power would you have and why?

- If you could do anything your heart desired, what would you do?

- What could be different in your life, right now, if you changed your thoughts?

- What does the perfect life mean to you?

- If you could be an animal, what animal would you be and why?

SOME ADDITIONAL QUESTIONS

- Who is in control of your life?

- What would the wisest part of yourself say to you right now?

- What advice would you give to the younger you? What advice would the older you give you now?

Use powerful questions to get to know a young person and learn more about who she is, or to help her get unstuck and shift her perception during coaching sessions. Young people might also wish to journal their responses to these questions.

Activity 1.19: My Future Self

Resources required   *Worksheet 25: My Future Self*

Activity aims   *To encourage positive perceptions of the future*
To explore the steps and actions necessary to create positive future change

This activity could be extended into a creative writing or arts activity, using the prompts in Worksheet 25.

Encourage the young person to project herself into her future self and describe how she looks, what she is doing in the future, and so forth. Avoid any negative descriptions at this stage, and encourage the young person to only identify positive attributes and descriptions. If necessary, use the young person's answers from earlier activities (such as the skills she identified she had in the Goal Setting Action Plan in Worksheet 12), to highlight how she is equipped and able to become this example in the future.

Depending on the age and ability level of the young person, and the appropriateness, explore whether she needs to change her current thoughts or behaviours to reach this positive version of herself in the future. You may wish to refer back to the negative habits the young person identified in Worksheet 22.

This activity can also link to goal setting. Encourage the young person to consider what current steps need to be taken to reach this positive version of her future self.

Activity 1.20: Vision Board

Resources required	Paper; scissors; glue; collage materials, including magazines and images
Activity aims	To create a positive life vision To create a visual reminder of goals and life purpose

Creating a vision board is a simple and fun way to set goals for the future. They are usually large collages depicting images to represent how people envision their future life to be. This can help people to set goals, to explore what they are working towards, to identify what is missing in their life at present, and serves as a visual reminder of their intentions for the future.

Gather some collage materials, including large sheets of paper, different magazines and newspapers or images from the internet. Encourage the young person to fill a sheet of paper with any words, phrases or images that describe something she wants to attain in the future.

You may wish to re-explore the young person's values, and what may underpin some of the tangible things they represent on her vision board. For example, a fast car might represent freedom, or holidays in exotic places may represent the value of adventure or independence.

There are no right or wrong ways to create a vision board. There are lots of online tools to create vision boards, which some young people may prefer to do. Encourage the young person to keep her vision board in a prominent place at home to help her stay on track with her goals.

✓

Worksheet 1
Checklist for Coaching

Initial session checklist

☐ Copies of worksheets including the Worksheet 10: General Scaling Tool to assess and measure progress.

☐ Permission has been granted for the young person to attend coaching from the parent or guardian (if needed).

☐ Quiet, semi-private space is available to conduct coaching sessions.

☐ Progress journal for young person to keep and record their thoughts and learning.

☐ Coach has copies of child protection and behaviour policies for school/setting.

☐ Aware of fire exits and procedures, and location of telephone, main office and first aid kit.

Final session checklist

☐ Post-coaching measurements have been completed using the General Scaling Tool to assess overall progress.

☐ Coaching Feedback Form (Worksheet 42) has been completed (if required).

☐ Additional support or worksheets identified for young people in need, including referrals for further support.

☐ Ending action plan is completed, highlighting the young person's progress and learning and creating future goals and actions post-coaching.

Worksheet 2
Coaching Appointment Reminder Cards

Coaching reminder card

Your next meetings are on:

.... at ....

.... at ....

.... at ....

Contact: _____

Coaching reminder card

Your next meetings are on:

.... at ....

.... at ....

.... at ....

Contact: _____

Coaching reminder card

Your next meetings are on:

.... at ....

.... at ....

.... at ....

Contact: _____

Coaching reminder card

Your next meetings are on:

.... at ....

.... at ....

.... at ....

Contact: _____

Coaching reminder card

Your next meetings are on:

.... at ....

.... at ....

.... at ....

Contact: _____

Coaching reminder card

Your next meetings are on:

.... at ....

.... at ....

.... at ....

Contact: _____

Life Coaching Action Plan

Name of young person:	
School/setting:	
Name of coach:	
Start date of intervention:	

Date:		**Session number**	

Focus of session:

Follow-up action/planned activities:

Worksheet 4
Weekly Progress Sheet

Name:		Date:		Session number:	

This week in coaching we discussed:

My goals and activities for next week are:

What has gone well this week:

Some of the challenges I've faced this week:

Wheel of Life

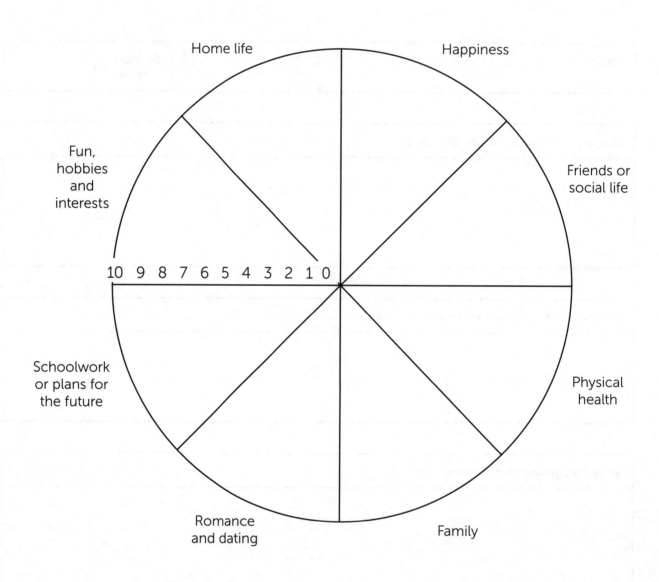

The parts of my life that need to improve are:

_____

_____

_____

_____

Connecting With Feelings

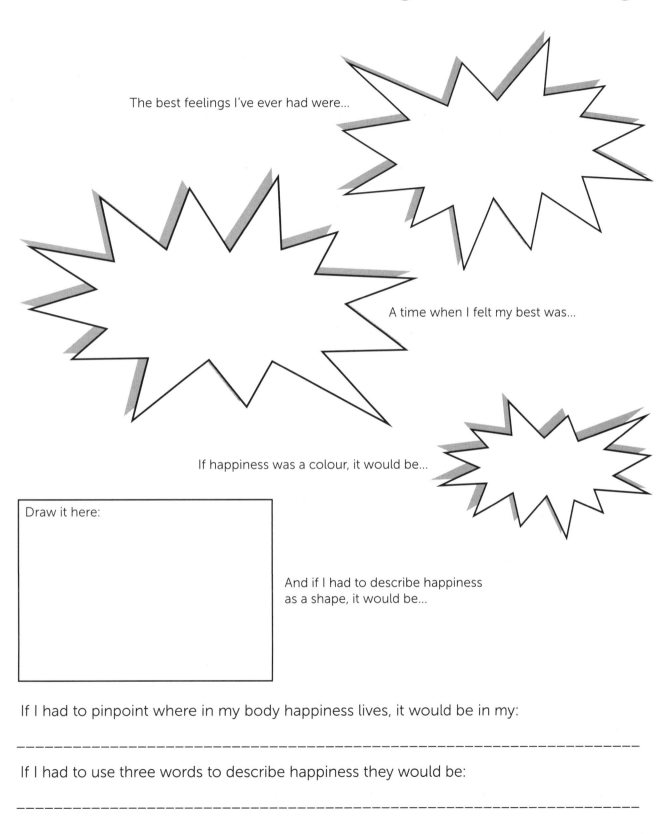

The best feelings I've ever had were...

A time when I felt my best was...

If happiness was a colour, it would be...

Draw it here:

And if I had to describe happiness
as a shape, it would be...

If I had to pinpoint where in my body happiness lives, it would be in my:

_____

If I had to use three words to describe happiness they would be:

_____

Worksheet 7
My Priorities

Look at each box below and write or draw any words that come to mind to when you think of that part of your life.

  For example, in the 'Friends' box you might write 'happy, play, fun, football' and so on. These might be positive or negative words. There are no right or wrong answers.

Friends	Family
Home	**School**
Hobbies and interests	**Other**

Looking at the boxes above, which parts of your life would you say are the most important to you?

Now, look at each box below and this time write how each part of your life makes you feel. It might be a good feeling, a bad feeling or a mixture. There are no right or wrong answers.

Some examples of positive feelings: happy, joyful, excited, calm, relaxed, cheerful, proud, important, safe, satisfied.

Some examples of negative feelings: sad, angry, upset, frustrated, confused, worried, anxious, embarrassed, scared, jealous.

Friends	Family
Home	School
Hobbies and interests	Other

Things That Are Important to Me

Think about all the different parts of your life and make a list of the things that are important to you. They might be people (like your best friend), activities (like swimming), places (like your home or a favourite city), things that make you feel good (like being with your grandmother, or going to school), or just words that describe important ideas (like independence, being in control, or having adventures). There are no right or wrong answers, just your thoughts and ideas.

Worksheet 9
Values List

Look at the list of words below and circle the ones that matter the most to you.

Feeling secure	Achieving something	Being in nature
Having freedom	Feeling peaceful	Feeling part of a community
Growing as a person	Feeling competitive	Beauty
Making a difference	Being popular	Health/fitness
Being confident	Loyalty	Love
Trust	Honesty	Having fun
Money	Learning new things	Friendship
Communication with others	Having adventures	Happiness
Being independent	Feeling fulfilled	Being alone
Feeling empowered	Being creative	Faith/belief in something

Now, pick your top ten words from the list above and write them in the first column below. Then rank them in order, from 1–10, with '1' being the thing that is the most important to you out of that list, and '10' being the least.

Finally, give a score from 1–10 in the third column to describe how satisfied you are that each thing that is important to you is being met in your life. For example, being independent is really important to you, but you don't feel you can make your own choices or follow your heart, so your level of satisfaction with independence is only 5 out of 10.

Top things I value	Rank (1–10)	Level of satisfaction

1. Where am I now?

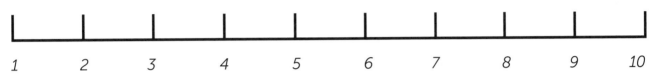

What does this look like? How do you know you're at that number?

2. Where do I want to be?

How would you know you were at that number?

3. How far have I come?

Goal Setting Brainstorming

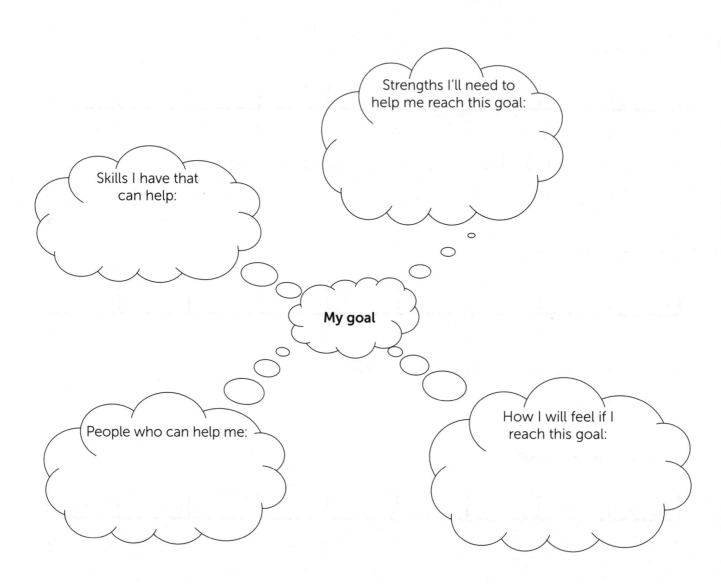

Goal Setting Action Plan

My goal is to...

Small steps I will take
to reach my main goal:

6.

5.

4.

3.

2.

1.

How will I know I've reached my goal?

✓

Keeping track of progress

Date	Progress	How close am I to my goal? (%)
----------	--------------------------------	----------
----------	--------------------------------	----------
----------	--------------------------------	----------
----------	--------------------------------	----------
----------	--------------------------------	----------
----------	--------------------------------	----------
----------	--------------------------------	----------
----------	--------------------------------	----------
----------	--------------------------------	----------
----------	--------------------------------	----------
----------	--------------------------------	----------
----------	--------------------------------	----------
----------	--------------------------------	----------
----------	--------------------------------	----------

My reward for reaching my goal will be:

Gains and Losses Worksheet

If I choose to _____

For myself:

Gains	Losses

For others:

Gains	Losses

Thoughts and Feelings Graph

Feelings

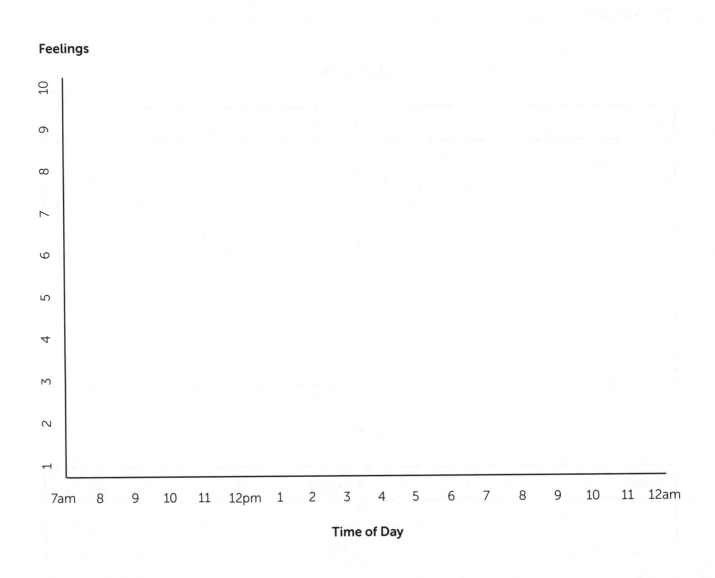

Time of Day

Thoughts, Feelings, Behaviours

Describe the situation you are struggling with. _____

_____

In the boxes below, write what you were **thinking** at the time, how you were **feeling**, and what you **did** (your actions).

Actions:

Thoughts:

Feelings:

Now, consider how you could change that situation. What thoughts could you think instead, to create better feelings and different actions?

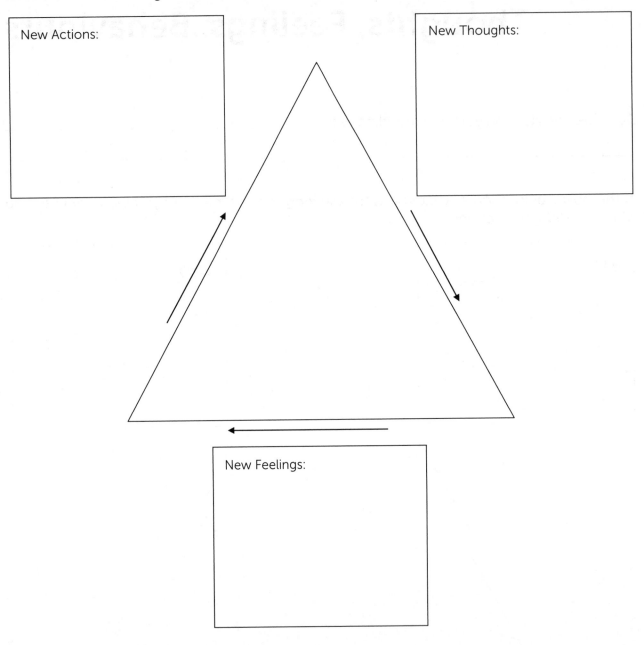

New Actions:

New Thoughts:

New Feelings:

How will things be different if I change my thoughts about this situation?

Worksheet 16
Automatic Thoughts

Date	Situation	Feelings	Automatic thoughts	Possible alternatives	Results
	What happened, or what were you thinking about?	*How did you feel inside?* *How bad was the feeling? (1–10)*	*What thoughts popped into your mind? How much did you believe them? (1–10)*	*What could be alternative thoughts you could think? How much do you believe them? (1–10)*	*How do you feel now? What action will you take now?*

Belief Labels

I am a good person	I deserve good things in my life
I am beautiful, inside and out	I am pretty and attractive
People like me	I am accepted for who I am
I am wanted	I am intelligent
I am good at certain things	I have a great future ahead of me

The world is a safe place	Life is fun
I am creative	I am talented
I have something to contribute to the world	Life is an adventure
I am healthy and strong	Exciting things are in my future
I am confident	My thoughts and opinions are valued

I am not good enough	I need to change how I look
I am not pretty enough	I am dumb
There's nothing I'm good at	I am stuck where I am
The world is unsafe and dangerous	People are out to get you
I am weak	I am not confident

140

Nothing good will happen to me	I can't make positive changes in my life
Life is hard work	People don't like me
People wouldn't like me if they knew the real me	I need to keep people at arm's length
It's dangerous to let people get too close to you	I am different to others
People don't respect me	People will only like me if I give them what they want

Worksheet 18
Challenging Limiting Beliefs

Unhelpful belief	*For example, 'I believe I am ugly'*
Reasons why I don't want to believe this is true	*For example, 'I feel bad about myself when I think I'm ugly. It makes me upset, I don't like going out with my friends. I feel like everyone is better than me'*
Reasons why I might want to believe this is true	*For example, 'When I think I'm ugly it stops me from trying new things and meeting new people which scares me. My friends give me sympathy when I say stuff about my looks'*
A new, positive thought I could believe in	*For example, 'I am unique and special, just the way I am'*

Changing Beliefs

Unhelpful belief	*For example, 'I believe I am stupid'*
Choose a number to describe how true this belief is for you Rate it from 1–100%, with 100% being completely true	*I believe I'm stupid, 99%*
Why might this belief not be true? What evidence can you find that makes you feel it might not be true?	*I got an 'A' on my science test; I am good at reading*
How much do you believe it to be true now? Rate it from 1–100%, with 100% being completely true	*I now believe I'm stupid, 50%*
What new, positive thoughts could you think to change that belief?	*I am good at some things. I have talents. I need help with some things but not all*
Choose a new, empowering belief	I have talents and strengths

Mood and Thought Record

Date		
Feelings	How do you feel inside? Rate it from 1–10.	
Thoughts	What thoughts are you thinking? How helpful are they from 1–10?	
Triggers	Did anything happen to trigger these thoughts or feelings?	

Worksheet 21
The Inner Critic

The unhelpful voice in our mind is sometimes called our 'inner critic'. It is a critical and sometimes mean voice that fills our head with unhelpful thoughts and leaves us feeling low.

My inner critic's name is: _____

He or she looks like...

My inner critic is fond of saying things like...

_____
_____
_____
_____
_____
_____
_____
_____
_____
_____
_____

I'm going to replace my inner critic with: _____

He or she looks like...

Who is fond of saying positive things like:

_____
_____
_____
_____
_____
_____
_____
_____
_____
_____
_____

Daily Habits

It is easy to get into habits of behaving a certain way on a day-to-day basis. Sometimes these habits are positive, like drinking lots of water each day or setting our alarm clock so we're not late. Sometimes these habits can be negative, often without us realizing, such as smoking, making fun of people, or thinking that we're not good enough.

Write down some of your positive and negative habits below. Remember that habits are not just obvious things we do, like skipping school. They can be thoughts, or subtle behaviours.

	Positive habits		Negative habits
1		1	
2		2	
3		3	
4		4	
5		5	
6		6	
7		7	
8		8	
9		9	
10		10	

The Magic Question

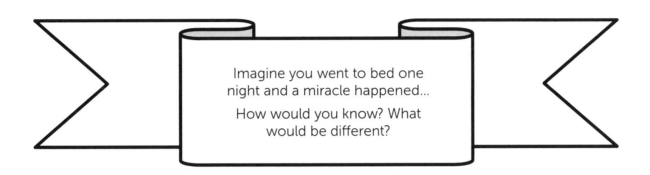

Imagine you went to bed one
night and a miracle happened...

How would you know? What
would be different?

✓

Powerful Questions

If you could wave a magic wand, what would you change about your life?

If you could have a **super power**, what power would you have and **why**?

What is the **BEST** thing about being you?

What could be different in your life, right now, if you changed your thoughts?

What does the perfect life mean to you?

If you could do anything your heart desired, what would you do?

If you could be an animal, what animal would you be and why?

My awesome future self looks like...

Sounds like...

Is doing...

The steps I need to take to get to my awesome future self are...

Theme 2

Relationships

Activity 2.1: Circle of Influence

Resources required *Worksheet 26: Circle of Influence*

Activity aims *To identify the people in a young person's life*
To create a support system for young people
To help identify the people who can support and help young people
to reach their goals

Worksheet 26: Circle of Influence encourages a young person to identify the various people in his life who form his support system. This helps to acknowledge the breadth of support in his life.

- Starting in the top circle, ask the young person to write the names of all the people who are the closest to him – family, best friends, etc.

- In the next circle, he should write the names of people who are next closest – perhaps friends in school, people he hangs out with, extended family members.

- In the final circle, he should write the names of other people in his life – acquaintances perhaps, classmates, people who drift in and out of his life or who are only occasionally present. There will be lots of people in this circle, so he can choose to just write a few names as examples.

When complete, explore how each group would describe the young person, focusing on his positive attributes, talents and skills. This activity can help the young person to become aware of the different levels of friendship and support in his life, and who he can lean on when needed.

Activity 2.2: Relationship Values

Resources required   *Worksheet 27: Relationship Values*

Activity aims   *To help young people define the values and qualities their relationships should embody*
To identify unsupportive or unresourceful relationships

This activity is suited to older young people (approximately aged 12+).

Explore Worksheet 27: Relationship Values, and discuss the concept of both relationships and values, that is:

- Our relationships can include anyone we spend time with, from people we are close to, such as good friends or family, to acquaintances or people who are paid to be in our life, like teachers.

- Our values are things that are important to us.

Discuss with the young person the idea of our relationships providing us with feelings and experiences that are important to us. Brainstorm some ideas to describe the values our relationships might reflect, such as trust, freedom, independence, fun, safety, communication, reliability, and so on.

Ask the young person to list those important values in the first column on the worksheet, and rank them in order from the most important, to the least. Next, work together to define how satisfied he is that each thing he values is being met in his life at present, and which people might provide that for him. For example, trust in relationships might be the number one quality that is important to the young person, but he doesn't feel he can trust anyone except his dad.

Use the worksheet as a discussion prompt, exploring the quality of the young person's relationships. Are any of the relationships unhelpful or damaging? Who are the people who provide the most support that might be helpful when trying to reach goals?

Activity 2.3: Memory Book

Resources required   *A small notebook; scissors; glue; collage materials; marker pens*

Activity aims   *To explore and preserve an important relationship*

This is a useful activity for a young person who has lost someone significant to him, or wishes to preserve the memory of someone. Use your judgement to determine the right time to create a memory book, and offer the idea to the young person as a suggestion, allowing him to decide if he wants to proceed.

There are no rules for what a memory book should be – for some it is a collection of photographs, while others use a scrapbook approach. Others choose to mix photographs with drawings, journaling, poems or special quotes. Many online companies now offer tools to create digital photo albums or memory books, which is another option for children who enjoy using technology or who may want multiple copies of their memory book.

Encourage communication by talking to the young person as he creates his book. Be open to hearing his thoughts as he goes through the process and be prepared to provide physical and emotional support as necessary.

When the memory book is complete, find a special place to keep it that is private yet easily accessible to the young person. Some may wish to share their creation, whilst others will want to keep their memories private.

EXTENSION ACTIVITY

The memory book approach can also be used to help a young person express his reflections on and memories of his own life. This may be useful for a young person suffering from low self-esteem or with a complex personal history. Work alongside him to explore ideas to include in his book, drawing on his strengths, talents, achievements and values to include within the book, as well as his memories. The book can also be added to in the future, linking to goal setting. The child may wish to include their goals and achievements, for example, when completing activities such as Activity 1.7: Goal Setting.

Activity 2.4: The Wise Friend

Resources required   *Worksheet 28: The Wise Friend; sheet of paper; pens*

Activity aims   *To build positive self-talk*
To build awareness of the young person's internal voice and patterns of thinking

Explain the concept of internal voice to the young person – the thoughts and 'voice' in our head that create positive or negative thoughts when we or someone else does or says something. Sometimes this voice is helpful and positive, and sometimes it is negative.

Worksheet 28: The Wise Friend helps young people to develop the idea of creating a positive, affirming and friendly internal voice. Discuss the idea of having a wise, caring friend, and identify some ideas of how that friend might treat the young person, and what the friend might say in difficult situations.

Complete the worksheet, and share the following examples, if needed:

- Consider a negative event happening, like someone calling you a name in the school hallway. A positive and optimistic voice inside might think: 'I'm really upset she just called me fat, but she does it to all the girls who aren't in her group. I know I'm not fat and she's just lashing out at me.'

- A negative voice inside might think: 'How embarrassing, everyone heard that. I can't believe she called me fat. But she's right, I am fat. I bet everyone starts calling me fat now. She always picks on me, it's not fair.'

Help the young person to identify some phrases she could repeat and focus on if needed, such as 'You're okay' or 'There's a solution to every problem.' Write them down so the young person can keep them to hand.

Activity 2.5: Forgiveness

Resources required	*Worksheet 29: Forgiveness Script; a quiet space*
Activity aims	*To explore the concept of forgiveness*
	To help young people reframe their interactions with others
	To create a positive outlook

Forgiveness is a concept that many young people can struggle with. Forgiving someone can feel like condoning or accepting their behaviour, or being in a position of weakness. This activity helps young people to reframe their ideas about forgiveness, and to let go of heavy emotions that may be holding them back.

Ensure the young person is in a safe and quiet space, and spend some time helping him to relax and feel at ease. Practise breathing techniques or just encourage the young person to be still and quiet for a few moments.

When ready, ask the young person to close his eyes and imagine he is seated in a large room opposite a big TV screen. He has the remote control for the TV in his hand and can change the channel, pause, fast-forward, rewind or stop at any time by pressing the buttons.

Read aloud the script in Worksheet 29, using a calm, soft tone of voice. Read the script slowly, pausing to allow the young person to visualize as you read. Be ready to stop if the young person appears uncomfortable or agitated. The script asks the young person to visualize various people in his life appearing on the TV screen, and gives the opportunity to visualize forgiving them for any wrongdoing, and receiving forgiveness. At the end of the script the young person visualizes the people in his life 'stepping out of the TV screen' to surround him with love and support.

When complete, allow the young person to reflect upon the process for a few moments, before encouraging him to open his eyes and stretch, slowly coming back into the room.

Discuss his responses to the process and any particular reflections or realizations he had. The young person can repeat this process at any time.

Circle of Influence

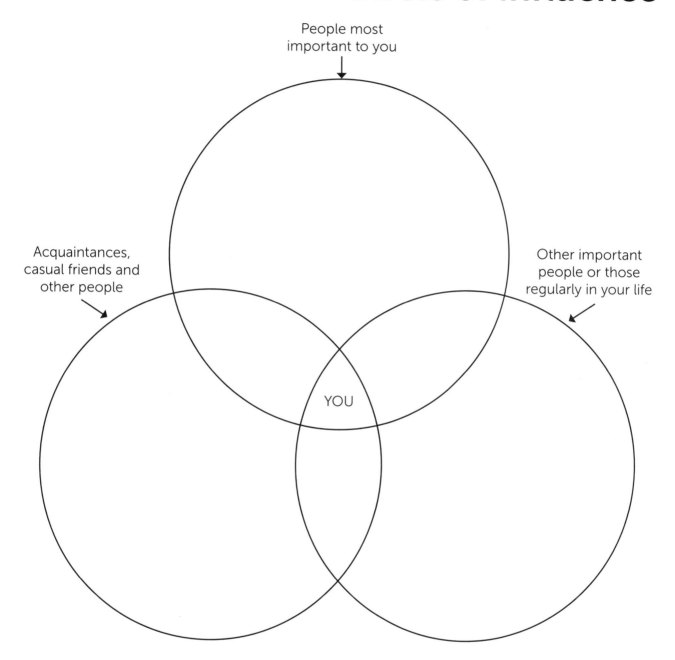

People most
important to you

Acquaintances,
casual friends and
other people

Other important
people or those
regularly in your life

YOU

What would each group say about you?

What positive words might they use to describe you?

✓

Relationship Values

Things that are important to me that need to be reflected in my relationships	Rank	Level of Satisfaction (1–10)	Which relationships do I have that include these things right now?
For example, independence	2	3/10	With my best friend
For example, trust	1	2/10	Sometimes with my mum

How can I get these important things met in my relationships?

Are there any relationships I have that are not providing me with the things I need?

Worksheet 28
The Wise Friend

Sometimes we think or say things to ourselves that aren't very helpful. Sometimes we notice ourselves doing it, and other times we don't. Take a minute to stop and listen to the voice inside, and see if that voice is actually helpful or not. What is it saying? Is it making you feel better or worse? Is it a positive or negative voice?

You can easily turn your internal voice into that of a really helpful, supportive and loving friend who only wants what's best for you and who is always positive and optimistic – what could be better!

Think about what the wise friend would look and sound like.

Would they be gentle, supportive? What tone of voice would they use? List some aspects of your wise internal friend below.

Think about a negative event happening, for example, someone making a mean or nasty comment about you.

What would a wise friend say? How would they react?

Worksheet 29
Forgiveness Script

Read aloud the following visualization script using a calm, soft tone of voice. Be cautious when completing this exercise if you feel it might be traumatic for the young person to try a forgiveness process – he may not be ready or able to forgive someone for hurt or pain they've caused. You might instead want to give the young person a copy of this script so he can read and undertake the process himself, at his own rate.

Close your eyes and relax. Notice your breathing getting slower and slower, deeper and deeper. Feel your body start to uncurl and relax.

Imagine you are seated in a big, comfortable chair in your favourite room. You feel relaxed and at ease, curled up in a soft chair in this happy, safe place. In front of you is a big TV screen – it's so big it fills the whole wall, and you have the remote control for the TV in your hands. You know you are in complete control of what appears on this TV and can switch it off at any time.

In your mind, press a button on the remote control and bring the TV to life. In a moment you can invite anyone who has hurt, upset or wronged you to appear on the TV so they can apologize to you. Each person wants to ask for your forgiveness, and tell you how much they care about you. Some of these people might have a special message to help you.

When you are ready, press a button on the remote control and see the first person's face on the TV. Remember, you are in control of the TV and can pause or stop at any time. Take your time to see this person's face. Their eyes are full of love and care for you. They are asking for your forgiveness, and you can see how genuine they are. Take a moment to listen to what they say if you want to.

(Pause for a moment to let the child visualize this.)

If you feel ready and able, you can choose to forgive this person in your mind for whatever it is they've done to you, knowing that forgiveness doesn't mean forgetting or pretending everything is okay. By forgiving them you are letting go of the hurt and bad feelings you've kept inside. Take a moment to feel that forgiveness in your body if you are ready to do so, and feel that big weight lifting off your shoulders. Listen to hear if they have a message for you. Take a deep breath and let those hurt feelings slip away as you breathe out.

(Pause for a moment to let the child visualize this.)

When you are ready you can press fast forward and invite another person to show up on the TV. Take some time to see each person in your life who is asking for your forgiveness. Notice how much they care for you and love you and how good it feels to let go of your anger and hurt. Listen to hear if they have some kind, encouraging words for you. Feel that upset and anger slip away each time you breathe out.

(Pause for a longer moment to let the child visualize this.)

Now when you're ready, you can invite anyone *you* have ever wronged or hurt to appear on the TV screen, so you can apologize and be forgiven. Take a moment to see those people appear. They are smiling and happy, full of love for you. They only want what's best for you and you can see any bad feeling that was there just floating away.

(Pause for a longer moment to let the child visualize this.)

Now, when you are ready, and if you choose to do so, you can press the special button on the remote control that will allow all those people who love and care about you to step out of the TV and into the room, so they can surround you with love and support.

If you want to, and when you're ready, press that special button and see all those people who care about you appearing around you. Look how happy they are to be with you. They're cheering and clapping for you – they know what an amazing person you are. Some of them might be telling you how proud they are of you or giving you some special words of encouragement. Notice how good it feels to be you right now, with all that love and support surrounding you. Notice how light and joyful your body feels right now.

You know you can call upon these feelings at any time and remember how it feels to be here.

When you are ready, press the button on the remote control again and watch as the TV powers down. You know you can return to this special room at any time.

Coming back to the here-and-now with all those lovely, supportive feelings, slowly start to wriggle your body and stretch, opening your eyes, and bring yourself back in this room.

Theme 3
Self-Image

Activity 3.1: Self-Talk

Resources required	*Worksheet 30: Self-Talk; scissors; marker pens; yarn; small pegs or paperclips*
Activity aims	*To explore the concept of self-talk* *To identify positive and negative examples of self-talk*

Make copies of Worksheet 30 so that each young person has at least 10–15 speech bubbles.

Explore the concept of self-talk – the voice inside our mind that chatters away. Sometimes we are aware of this voice and sometimes not.

Cut out the speech bubbles and create a 'washing line' by stringing up a length of yarn across the room. Ask the young person to write down on each speech bubble some examples of thoughts that go through her mind when:

- she looks in the mirror

- she is with her friends

- she is at home

- she is alone.

Stress that there are no right or wrong answers, and some of the thoughts may be positive, and some may be negative.

When ready, ask the young person to peg or tape the speech bubbles to the washing line, with negative thoughts on the right-hand side, and positive thoughts on the left-hand side.

Discuss whether there are more positive or negative speech bubbles, and ask the young person to choose a few that most bother her.

Using blank speech bubbles, work together to create positive examples of self-talk to counteract these thoughts. Encourage the young person to say the phrases out loud, and if appropriate, try saying them into a mirror.

Activity 3.2: Being Me

Resources required	Worksheet 31: Being Me
Activity aims	To explore different roles and ways of being
	To encourage young people to live authentically and be true to themselves
	To identify unresourceful patterns of behaviour and interaction with others

This activity explores the concept of the different roles people can play or the masks they can wear that hide their true, authentic self.

Review Worksheet 31: Being Me and discuss the three versions of 'The fake me', 'The negative me' and 'The real me'. Discuss how we all, at times, can play a role or pretend to be something we're not, because we are afraid of people's reactions or that people won't like the real us. Provide some examples to help the young person understand if necessary, such as the person who pretends to be rebellious and a troublemaker because they are afraid to lose control or they are afraid people will think they're weak.

Encourage the young person to complete the three boxes with words or images and discuss the results.

DISCUSS WITH THE YOUNG PERSON

- Which parts of you are not helpful, or not working?

- How can you be more real?

- How can you share more of the real you with the world?

- What's the worst thing that could happen if you were 'real' with people?

Activity 3.3: Mind Movies

Resources required	*A quiet space*
Activity aims	*To create a positive sense of self-image*
	To help young people connect with the positive attributes of their physical being
	To create positive patterns of thinking, related to self-image

Use this simple visualization activity to help a young person with poor self-image to create a positive picture in her mind of her body or appearance. This process can then be repeated at any time to help strengthen the young person's perception of her self-image.

Encourage the young person to find a comfortable position and to relax, focusing on her breathing. Read the following script slowly, in a soft tone of voice.

Close your eyes and relax. Notice your breathing getting slower and slower, deeper and deeper. Feel your body start to uncurl and relax.

Imagine in your mind that you are seated in a really comfortable chair, in a special room. You feel safe and at peace in this room. You know that no one will be disturbing you – this is your space.

In your hands you have a large photograph of you. Look at the photo and take in the details of your face and body. You look so happy and carefree, your smile is wide and your eyes are sparkling. Notice how strong your body looks, and how confident you appear. Look at the details of what you're wearing and how you're standing. You've never seen yourself looking so beautiful and full of joy.

As you look at the photograph, notice how bright it's becoming. All the colours are getting brighter and brighter; the photograph is getting bigger in your hand.

Now, imagine you are going to take three deep breaths and blow them onto the photograph. One...two...three. Nice big breaths that are breathing life into the photograph. Notice now how the image is coming to life, you can see yourself moving in the photo and hear yourself laughing. The you in the photograph is getting larger...now they are standing in front of you. If you want to, you can step into that version of you. Imagine you are getting out of the chair in your safe space, and stepping into the body of that happy, confident you. Notice how it feels to be you. You feel light and relaxed, carefree and joyful. Your body feels strong, healthy and powerful. You love being in this wonderful body that can help you do so many things.

Now, when you are ready, you can step back out and sit back in the chair, keeping all those lovely feelings with you. You know you can call on those feelings at any time, and remember what it's like to feel so strong and healthy at any time.

Slowly come back into your body in the here and now. Flex your fingers and toes and give your body a big stretch if you need to. When you are ready, open your eyes.

DISCUSS WITH THE YOUNG PERSON

- How did it feel to see that happy, healthy version of you?

- How did it feel to step into that body?

- Do you think you can keep those feelings with you?

Note: The young person can repeat this visualization at any time on her own, adding more detail to embed the imagery and sensation of this healthy version of herself. You may need to repeat the script over a number of sessions to help some young people become accustomed to the process.

Activity 3.4: Mirror, Mirror

Resources required	*Worksheet 32: Mirror, Mirror*
Activity aims	*To identify positive attributes and features related to self-image* *To acknowledge positive qualities about the young person's body and physical appearance*

This simple activity can be used to assist a young person with a negative self-image or who has low self-esteem.

Use the mirror shape in Worksheet 32 to encourage the young person to write or draw how she and others see her. Help the young person to identify positive attributes and encourage her to identify qualities other people might see in her, as well as physical attributes.

Extend this activity by reproducing the worksheet on a larger scale and using collage materials or paint to draw the young person's positive attributes, or explore the positives of different parts of her body, for example, her eyes help her to see; her legs are strong and help her to run and dance, etc.

Being Me

Sometimes we hide the real us behind a mask – we pretend to be something we're not, because we're afraid people won't like the real us. Think about how you might describe the three versions of you. An example is provided to help you start.

The fake me	**The negative me**	**The real me**
Sometimes I pretend to be…	Sometimes I'm afraid I am…	Who I really am is…
popular and cool, hanging out with the 'cool kids' and doing stuff like smoking to fit in	*boring and geeky…too boring for people to want to be friends with me*	*a caring, thoughtful person, a good friend, a fun person*

Think about all the beautiful parts that make you. What do you see when you look in the mirror? What do other people see when they look at you? List or draw them in the mirror below.

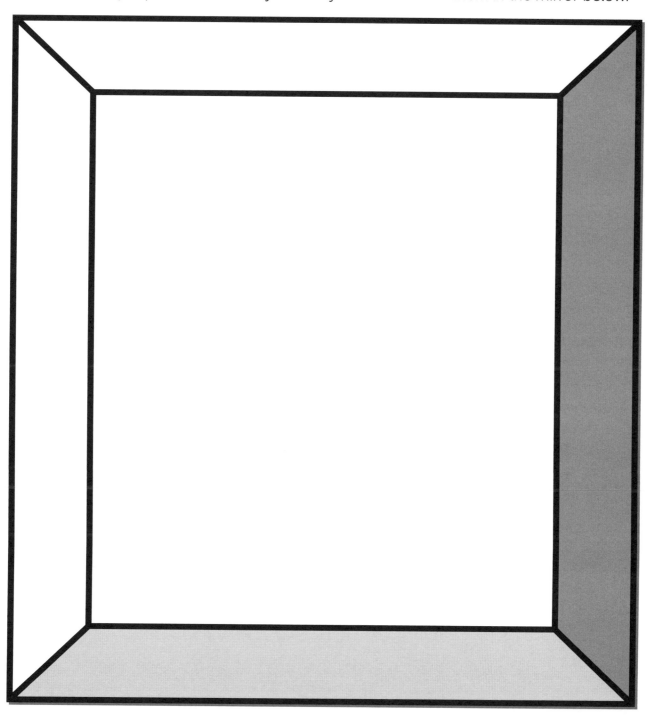

Theme 4

Bullying

Activity 4.1: The Superhero

Resources required   *Plain paper; marker pens; crayons; pencils*

Activity aims   *To identify coping mechanisms to manage bullying*

Children who experience persistent bullying can often become disempowered and entrenched in a negative mindset, devaluing their own attributes and assuming that the bullying is somehow their fault.

This activity helps to acknowledge children's inner resources to cope and manage incidents of bullying, and can be useful to help young people recover their self-esteem, once the bullying has stopped. Typically this activity is better suited to younger children.

Using drawing or painting materials ask the young person to create an anti-bullying superhero, imagining if such a superhero existed how he or she might look, what powers they might have, how they might stop bullying and promote friendship, etc. Spend some time drawing and labelling the superhero, thinking about which parts of the hero might represent a way to effectively respond to bullying, such as a shield to deflect comments, or powers to fly away from negative situations.

When complete spend some time discussing the superhero with the child, and begin to explore the child's 'powers' to stop bullying. Make a list of the child's responses to the questions below.

DISCUSS WITH THE CHILD

- What strengths and skills do you have to stop bullying?

- What powers do you have inside that can help you to cope (for example, positive thinking, laughing it off, telling someone about the bullying, deflecting verbal comments, etc.)?

- What 'power' could you use if someone called you a nasty name? Threatened you? Laughed at you?

Note: You may wish to create a simple visualization script using the child's superhero to help him embody the strength and positivity of his character.

Activity 4.2: The Shield

Resources required	*A quiet space*
Activity aims	*To create coping mechanisms for dealing with verbal or emotional bullying*
	To build a positive mindset to deflect bullying comments and teasing

This visualization helps young people experiencing bullying or teasing to deflect comments and to gain some control in negative situations. It can be used at any time by the young person, and for a variety of other situations, for example, when parents are arguing at home.

Encourage the young person to find a comfortable sitting position and to relax, focusing on his breathing. Read the following script slowly, in a soft tone of voice.

Close your eyes and relax. Notice your breathing getting slower and slower, deeper and deeper. Feel your body start to uncurl and relax.

Imagine in your mind that you have a large shield in your hand. It's a very special shield, shiny and gold. The edges of the shield are covered in special jewels – rubies, emeralds, diamonds and sapphires. You can see the reds and greens of the precious stones twinkling in the light, and the gold of the shield sparkles when the sun hits it.

Pick up the shield and hold it close to you. The shield is very thick and solid, but it feels light in your hands. You can easily hold it up in front of you – it's so big it covers your whole body.

This is a very special shield as it will protect you in any situation. Any time a person makes a nasty comment or throws a mean look or laughter in your direction, the shield will make it bounce off! Practise holding up the shield now and imagine someone has said something mean. The shield is huge – the mean comments bounce and fly right off, before they can reach you. Notice how special gold rays of light spread out from the shield, making you feel safe and protected. You only feel happy and confident – nothing bad can get around this shield.

Now imagine you can shrink this shield down to a tiny size, small enough to put in your pocket. Imagine placing it in your pocket now and feeling it close. You know you can always take it out and make it bigger again, whenever you need it.

Notice how safe and in control you feel. Now, when you are ready, you can start to come back to the here-and-now, keeping those lovely feelings with you.

Slowly come back into your body, flexing your fingers and toes, and give your body a big stretch if you need to. When you are ready, open your eyes.

Note: You may wish to use the imagery of a shield for younger children, and the idea of creating a bubble around themselves for older children. The bubble works in the same way, with the young person imagining that he has a giant bubble around himself. He is safe inside the bubble, and only positive comments and feelings can get through. Negative words, feelings, looks and so on bounce off the bubble.

Young people can use this imagery at any time, in any situation. Encourage them to practise using their shield or bubble (or both) whenever they need to.

Activity 4.3: Reframing Bullying

Resources required	*Worksheet 33: Reframing Bullying*
Activity aims	*To help a young person positively reframe unhelpful comments or verbal taunts*
	To prevent a young person from internalizing mean and bullying comments as beliefs

This activity can be used with young people who are verbally taunted by others, or who have received mean remarks and teasing from their peers. This activity can also be used to reframe unhelpful comments from parents, siblings and so on.

Reframing is the process of changing the meaning we place on something, to change its potency or to change how we respond to it – our thoughts, feelings and behaviours.

Worksheet 33 helps young people to identify some of the unhelpful comments, taunts or messages received from others. These can either be specific, such as someone recently saying they aren't cool enough to be their friend, or more general such as 'People say I'm ugly', which can be represented in a number of ways.

Work with the young person to list on the worksheet a few examples of unhelpful or negative comments she has received. Next, work together to identify new ways to challenge these comments, creating positive alternatives and finding the evidence as proof. For example:

People say to me: 'You are ugly.'

In reality I am: 'A beautiful person. I look pretty when I wear my hair up. I have nice eyes.'

I know this is true because: 'My mum tells me I'm pretty. I feel good when I look in the mirror. My best friend says she wishes she had my eye colour.'

Make a list of the reframed comments for the young person to keep and refer to when needed, or encourage her to write the positive comments in her journal each night or when she feels she needs an emotional boost.

Activity 4.4: Being Assertive

Resources required	*Worksheet 34: Being Assertive; scissors*
Activity aims	*To understand and identify the young person's response style*
	To build awareness and understanding of how to embody an assertive response style

Young people who are victims or perpetrators of bullying can often become locked in passive or aggressive patterns of behaviour respectively. This activity can help a young person to identify the qualities of a passive, aggressive and assertive person, shifting his behaviour to a confident, assertive standpoint.

Cut up the labels in Worksheet 34 and match each description with either the passive, aggressive or assertive person, placing the labels in the correct column. When complete, discuss the following points:

- Which position describes you best: passive, aggressive or assertive?

- How does it feel to be in that position?

- Which position would you like to get to (that is, assertive)?

- How can you become more assertive?

Help the young person to describe how he would think, feel, act as an assertive person, including how he would interact with others and what he might say. You may wish to extend this activity by using the body outline in Worksheet 40, and drawing or labelling the worksheet to describe how they could portray the young person's assertiveness through body language, facial expressions, speech, etc.

Model these patterns of speech, behaviours, body language and so forth for the young person, and encourage him to do the same, practising how to be assertive. This might form part of an action plan or homework as he practises his assertiveness in the 'real world'.

Activity 4.5: A Safe Place

Resources required	*A quiet place*
Activity aims	*To create a positive frame of mind*
	To encourage the young person to connect with feelings of safety and control as needed

This visualization is particularly suited for young people experiencing bullying, but can also be applicable for any child experiencing trauma, worries, anxiety, stress, and so forth.

Encourage the young person to find a comfortable sitting position and to relax, focusing on his breathing. Read the following script slowly, in a soft tone of voice.

Close your eyes and relax. Notice your breathing getting slower and slower, deeper and deeper. Feel your body start to uncurl and relax.

Imagine in your mind that you are in a very special place. It is a garden, filled with beautiful flowers and trees. It's a very safe garden, just for you. You can feel a gentle breeze and the warm sun touching your skin, and hear water bubbling over rocks in a small stream. Smell how sweet the flowers are. This really is a beautiful place; you feel so relaxed and happy in this garden that's just for you.

You notice a pathway through the garden and decide to follow it. There's a little bridge over the steam and you stop to lean on the bridge, taking a big deep breath of air into your lungs. You feel so relaxed and at ease. Your body feels light and you skip across the path, listening to the birds singing in the trees. Everything seems to sparkle and glow in the sunlight.

As you walk over the bridge and down the path you come to a gate. On the other side of the gate is a special place that's just for you. No one else can come into this place unless you invite them. It is your place to feel relaxed and happy and to do whatever you want. Open the gate and walk towards this lovely place that's just for you. Notice how your body feels in this place – so confident, healthy and strong. Your mind feels positive and clear of worries. You can be whoever you want to be in this place, you are totally safe.

You notice an animal is coming forward. This is a special animal, with a message for you. Look at the animal and notice what message they are giving to help you. What strengths does it hold that it wants you to have? By being near the animal you are soaking up all its special powers and strengths.

When you are ready, walk back through the gate and along the path, over the bridge and into the garden. You are bringing with you all of those lovely feelings of being in such a special, safe place, and you have the important message from your animal.

Now, when you are ready, you can start to come back to the here-and-now, keeping those lovely feelings with you.

Slowly come back into your body, flexing your fingers and toes, and give your body a big stretch if you need to. When you are ready, open your eyes.

Discuss with the young person

- How did it feel to be in your special place?

- Where in your body could you feel those nice feelings?

- What did your special place look like? (if they wish to share)

- What animal came to you? What message did it have for you (if they wish to share)?

- What qualities and strengths do you think your animal wanted you to have?

Note: As with other visualizations, the child can repeat this process at any time, for example, before going to sleep each night. He can add more detail, and invite a special person to come into the space if he wishes. The young person can connect with his safe place whenever he feels threatened, anxious or low.

Activity 4.6: Bully Mind Movies

Resources required	*A quiet place*
Activity aims	*To create a disassociation from negative people*
	To break the thought patterns of fear or intimidation associated with certain people

People who bully or intimidate can often become a threatening and overpowering image in a young person's mind. The more he focuses on the person, the bigger the threat appears. Their influence can become exaggerated by the mind, making them appear far more frightening or hurtful than they really are.

This activity is similar to Activity 3.3: Mind Movies, except in reverse. Instead of making the image in the mind larger and brighter (and therefore more significant), the young person will diminish the power of their internal perceptions, thus diminishing the impact of the thoughts and therefore the hurtful person.

Ensure the young person feels safe and able to complete this activity first, then follow the process below, asking the young person to sit comfortably and to close his eyes.

Think of the person who is bullying or hurting you, and see the person's face in your mind.

Imagine you are seeing that person on a large TV screen in front of you. You have the remote control for the TV in your hands.

Press pause and see the person's face paused in front of you.

Now press a button on the remote control and imagine the picture is turning black and white if it was in colour before.

Press another button now and imagine the picture is shrinking, shrinking, shrinking, until it is tiny!

Press another button and imagine the picture is so big you can't see the person's face any more; it's just blurry shapes.

Now shrink it down again and send it into the far corner of the TV screen.

Press play on the remote control and imagine the picture is coming to life, but the person is now wearing a big pink wig and a red nose.

Imagine their voice is getting squeakier and squeakier!

Finally, press stop and see the picture disappear into nothing.

The young person can repeat this process at any time, whenever he feels the need to diminish a person's internal influence. He can also play with the process, adding different silly voices or outfits to reduce the impact of a person. He may have to repeat it several times to change the association with the person into something more benign.

DISCUSS WITH THE YOUNG PERSON

- How did it feel to be in control of how you saw the person?

- How do you feel about the person now?

- What thoughts might you think to yourself when you think of this person now (for example, 'They can't hurt me'; 'I'm in control'; 'I am safe', etc.)?

Reframing Bullying

Sometimes when people say mean and nasty things to us we can start to believe them and think that what they say is true. Take some time to think about the unhelpful things people say to you, and write down the truth in the second column. Finally, write down some examples of evidence to prove that your positive thoughts are true.

Some people say to me...	In reality I am...	I know this is true because...
For example, 'I'm stupid and ugly'	*For example, 'A good person to know, I am smart and pretty'*	*For example, 'I scored A's on my test last week and my best friend tells me I'm pretty'*

Being Assertive

	A passive person	An aggressive person	An assertive person
Description of the person			
Language they may use			
Behaviours they may use			
How they present themselves			

Not standing up for themselves – allowing others to choose for them and not expressing themselves clearly.	Quiet, doesn't speak up or goes along with the crowd. Sounds like 'I don't mind' or 'Whatever you think'.	No eye contact, looking down, shoulders hunched.
Using their power over others to get what they want, putting themselves first, controlling others.	Insults, commands, loud or threatening, speaking over people. Sounds like 'You listen to me'.	Staring, arms folded, standing in someone's personal space, intimidating stance.
Stands up for themselves without hurting others, acting with confidence and being clear and direct.	Speaks clearly and respectfully, confidently communicating their thoughts and feelings. Sounds like 'I feel hurt when you leave me out'.	Confident, shoulders held back, head up, direct eye contact, stands tall.
This person has no authority or doesn't care what happens. This person is weak.	This person is a scary person to know. I don't feel safe with them and can't trust them.	This person will be honest and accepting; they are a good communicator. I feel safe with them. They won't abuse my trust.

Theme 5
Confidence

Activity 5.1: Confidence Role-Play

Explore the meaning of 'confidence'. What does it look and feel like? Identify some attributes of confident people, exploring how they act and interact with others.

Ask the young person to select one or two people she knows who are truly confident. These might be people she knows in real life, or celebrities. Discuss what makes these people confident, making a list. Consider each of the following aspects:

- how they speak

- the way they carry themselves

- their body language and facial expressions

- how they talk to people and interact with others

- how they think.

When complete, make another list alongside to describe the young person under the same criteria. Identify differences between the two – for example, the confident person holds her head up high, whereas the young person walks around with her eyes cast down.

Model some of the confident actions for the young person, such as showing her how to walk confidently, sit with her shoulders back and head up, or greet someone confidently. Encourage the young person to practise these actions herself in the safety of the coaching space.

Agree on an action plan for the following week, encouraging the young person to identify which confidence actions she will try first. Keep the goals small and manageable, especially if the young person is very lacking in confidence. For example, the first week's challenge may be to look one person in the eye, or to walk to school with her head up and shoulders back. Make this challenge fun and exciting, stressing how capable the young person is of reaching this goal. Continue adding further confidence steps as she becomes more adept and comfortable with the process.

Activity 5.2: Confidence Scales

Resources required   *Worksheet 35: Confidence Scales; paper; pens*

Activity aims   *To define the young person's current level of confidence*
To set a confidence goal

This activity replicates the process of using a scaling tool (as shown in Activity 1.6), but with a specific focus on confidence.

Using Worksheet 35, follow the process below with the young person:

1. Identify on the scale of 1–10 how confident the young person is, where '1' is not confident at all, and '10' is super-confident.

2. Ask the young person to list underneath or on a separate piece of paper how she knows she is at that number. What are some of the situations or ways in which she is not confident? When does she feel confident?

3. Identify on the second scale how confident she would like to be, on a scale of 1–10. Try and make this realistic – jumping from a '1' to a '10' is quite a leap.

4. As for the previous scale, identify again how the young person would know they were at that new number. What would be different? How would she respond differently in situations or with specific people? Make a list of her responses.

5. Explore how the young person could move one or two steps along the scale, from her initial starting point, for example, from a '2' to a '3' or '4'. What small steps could she take to become a little bit more confident?

6. Make a plan of action, and if necessary, use Activity 5.1: Confidence Role-Play, to model some of the small steps.

7. Review the scale regularly, taking continuous regular, small, steps to help the young person reach her confidence goal.

8. Finally, use the last scale to measure how far the young person has come. List the skills and attributes the young person demonstrated or learned to help her along her way – skills she could transfer to other parts of her life.

Activity 5.3: Confident Me

Resources required	*Worksheet 36: Confident Me*
Activity aims	*To connect a young person with an experience of being confident*
	To anchor the feelings and behaviours of being confident in the here-and-now

Worksheet 36: Confident Me encourages young people to connect with a time when they felt confident.

Encourage the young person to explore the worksheet, considering how she looked and acted when she felt confident, what she said, how she interacted with others, her thoughts, feelings and what happened as a result of her confidence – the consequences of being confident. Encourage the young person to understand that confidence is a frame of mind that she can create and connect with at any time.

When the worksheet is completed, try Activity 5.4: Confidence Visualization to anchor those memories into the here-and-now for the young person. Alternatively, encourage the young person to write memories of other times when she was confident in her journal, and to practise visualizing or remembering the details of being this confident version of herself.

Activity 5.4: Confidence Visualization

> **Resources required** — *A quiet space*
>
> **Activity aims** — *To anchor the feelings and behaviours of being confident in the here-and-now*

Use the following visualization script to help a young person connect with feelings of confidence and anchor those feelings and resources to call upon them at any time. (See Chapter 11 for more on resource anchoring.) You may wish to use this activity after the previous activity of identifying a time when the young person felt confident.

Encourage the young person to find a comfortable sitting position and to relax, focusing on her breathing. Read the following script slowly, in a soft tone of voice.

Close your eyes and relax. Notice your breathing getting slower and slower, deeper and deeper. Feel your body start to uncurl and relax.

Imagine you are standing in a special room, inside a special house. No one is there but you, and you feel completely safe and relaxed. There is a huge mirror resting against one of the walls. Go up and look at it closely. It's far bigger than you are, and you notice it has a beautiful swirling, gold edge to it. The mirror is really polished and shiny.

Go closer and look into the mirror. You can see your reflection shining back. As you look into the mirror, remember a time when you felt confident, a time when you were the most confident you ever felt in your life. Nothing could go wrong, you felt so strong and capable. You were totally in control. Look in the mirror and see that confident you, now.

Notice how strong you look, and how happy. Look at your eyes, shining with confidence. Your body is standing tall and proud, your shoulders relaxed and your back is tall and straight. Your head is held high and you are smiling. Can you hear yourself talking? You sound perfectly confident and clear. Your whole body crackles with confidence.

The more you look at yourself in the mirror, the more you can feel that confidence in your body, now. Notice how strong you feel, and how peaceful inside. You feel totally safe and secure. Notice how your body feels, and the thoughts in your mind, telling you that you can do anything you set out to do.

Feel those lovely feelings, and when you're ready, imagine all those confident feelings are swirling together in front of you. They're forming a very special shape – it's a band for you to wear around your wrist. Imagine you are slipping it on to your wrist now. Every time you touch the band you can experience those confident feelings again. Try it now.

Now, when you are ready, you can start to come back to the here-and-now, keeping those lovely feelings with you. Your band is still around your wrist, and you know you can call on those feelings by touching the band at any time.

Slowly come back into your body, flexing your fingers and toes and give your body a big stretch if you need to. When you are ready, open your eyes.

DISCUSS WITH THE YOUNG PERSON

- How did that process feel?

- Could you see the confident you in the mirror?

- What colour and shape is the band around you wrist (if they wish to share)?

Encourage the young person to practise touching the brand on her wrist (the resource anchor) and calling upon those feelings again. She may need to repeat the process several times to fully anchor the confident feelings.

1. How confident am I?

What does this look like? How do you know you're at that number?

2. How confident do I want to be?

How would you know you were at that number?

3. How far have I come?

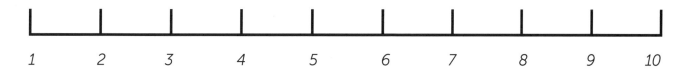

Confident Me

A time I was feeling my most confident was:

When I am confident my body feels like:

When I am confident I think these thoughts:

When I am feeling confident I look like this:

When I am confident I say things like...

Theme 6
Anxiety and Stress

Activity 6.1: Things That Make Me Feel...

Resources required   *Worksheet 37: Things That Make Me Feel Good or Bad*

Activity aims   *To build self-awareness about negative influences in life*
To avoid draining and negative activities that create stress and anxiety

This simple activity helps in identifying the people, activities and things that have a positive and negative impact on the well-being of a young person. By identifying potentially negative influences a young person can avoid or replace them.

Work with the young person to complete Worksheet 37: Things That Make Me Feel Good or Bad. These can be small things, like buying fashion magazines, or bigger things, like smoking or taking drugs. Encourage the young person to explore why those things make him feel bad and identify alternative behaviours that can have more positive results.

Activity 6.2: Gratitude Diary

Resources required   *Plain paper; pens*
Activity aims   *To create a positive outlook*

This activity can help a young person to manage feelings of stress, anxiety, worry or anger by focusing on the positives in his life. Although simple, this activity can be quite powerful, and can create shifts in thinking and perception.

On plain paper or in the young person's journal, encourage him to make a list of all the things he is grateful for. He can choose to write or draw the things he is grateful for, and even turn it into an arts exercise, creating a collage or painting. His gratitude list could include people, things he loves, places, memories, and so forth. Encourage him to reflect upon how it feels to have all those things in his life.

This can also be a very powerful daily exercise, creating a shift in perception.

Activity 6.3: Positive Thoughts

Resources required   *Worksheet 38: Positive Thoughts*

Activity aims   *To create positive thought patterns*
                            To reframe negative thoughts

This activity helps to create shifts in thinking, and to reframe thoughts more positively. It is particularly useful for young people whose stress, anxiety or worries are centred on their interactions with others, for example, arguments with parents, classmates they don't get along with, estranged family members, and so forth.

Using Worksheet 38: Positive Thoughts, discuss with the young person the people he is struggling to see in a positive light. List the names of those people in the left-hand column. Next, work together to identify positive thoughts to 'send' to those people, that is, something positive the young person would like to say to each person in real life, if he had the chance, or a thought that would help to change the way he feels about the person.

Explain to the young person that by choosing to think positive thoughts, he can change his perceptions of these people.

Activity 6.4: Affirmation Cards

Resources required   *Worksheet 39: Affirmation Cards; scissors*

Activity aims   *To create positive thought patterns*
To focus the mind and create a positive outlook

Affirmations are positively phrased, simple statements that if repeated often enough can create new patterns of thinking and perceptions and reframe negative core beliefs.

Affirmations are simple to create, and can be repeated by a person in his mind or aloud. Young people can choose to focus on one affirmation for a week, or choose a different daily affirmation, repeating the statement as often as they remember or need to.

Worksheet 39 contains a number of affirmation statements. Cut them up and either ask the young person to choose one at random, or choose one he is drawn to. The young person can either write the affirmation in his journal, or remember and repeat it to himself. Repeating the affirmation aloud, looking in the mirror, is particularly powerful.

To extend this activity, create affirmation cards using collage materials so the young person can keep the cards at home and refer to a new affirmation whenever he needs to.

Activity 6.5: Relaxation Techniques

Resources required   None

Activity aims   *To learn and practise a range of techniques to relax the body and mind*

Many children and young people are not taught how to relax their body or mind, or how to take control of their emotional state. Simple techniques such as those outlined below can help children stay in control when nerves or anxiety threaten to overcome them.

Model and teach these simple ways to relieve stress and keep calm, encouraging young people to practise them in their own time or when needed.

BREATHING TECHNIQUES

Start to breathe slowly and deeply, in a calm and effortless way. Starting with your feet, feel each part of your body relaxing, the tension seeping out as you work your way up to your face and head. As you focus on each area, notice how warm and heavy your body feels. Push any distracting thoughts to the back of your mind and imagine them floating away.

Inhale slowly and deeply, filling your chest with air, slowly counting four seconds to yourself. Imagine your chest slowly filling with air, from your diaphragm to your collarbone. Then, try and hold your breath for another four seconds, or less if this feels uncomfortable. Finally, gently exhale, letting the breath slide out slowly, all the way down to the lowest part of the lungs. Keep repeating until you feel more relaxed.

Close your eyes and imagine that you are holding a big balloon on your chest. As you breathe in feel the balloon gently rising up in the air. Imagine you are being gently lifted by the balloon into the sky. Your body feels light and weightless, as free as a bird. Each time you breathe gently in and out you rise higher into the sky, until you are ready to gently sail back to Earth.

MINDFULNESS

Mindfulness is a technique of focusing the mind and becoming aware in the present moment. Practise mindfulness by focusing the mind on the activity the body is engaged in, using all the senses to experience that moment. For example, if you are washing the dishes, pay attention to the feel of the water on your skin, the motion of the water as you use the dishcloth, how your body feels as you move your arm to wipe the plate clean, and so forth.

This activity can help to control the mind and stop a barrage of thoughts from bombarding a person, creating anxiety and confusion.

STRETCHING

Try simple stretches to ground and relax the body, such as the following:

- Place both feet together and stretching the arms forward, fold over at the waist. Try and touch your toes if possible.

- Stretch your arms over your head, pushing your fingers towards the ceiling.

- Lie on the floor and stretch your arms above your head. Stretch your legs and toes in the opposite direction.

- Crouch on all fours and reach forward with both arms, tucking your head in to stretch your back.

Encourage young people to create a dedicated 'relaxation time' once or twice a week. Create an environment for relaxation with a warm bath, or soft music, candles or incense (when supervised), or use soft lighting to create a relaxing mood. Encourage them to turn off phones and other electronic devices and to dedicate the time to de-stressing, thinking positive thoughts, resting the body or journaling.

Activity 6.6: Address the Stress

Resources required *Worksheet 40: Address the Stress*

Activity aims *To identify where stress and anxiety may be located in the body*
To identify ways in which to reduce stress

Using the body outline in Worksheet 40, work with the young person to identify where in his body he feels anxiety, stress, distress, worry and so forth. There are no right or wrong answers, and this may take some time to help the young person get in touch with his body and how it feels.

The young person can write or draw on the body outline the different feelings or sensations he experiences when feeling stressed or anxious, such as:

- tightness in the chest, jaw, neck or shoulders leading to shortness of breath, grinding of teeth or headaches

- tiredness and sleep problems

- feeling angry or upset

- worries and unwanted thoughts or mood swings

- not feeling hungry

- butterflies in the stomach

- aching muscles.

Younger children might want to use colours and patterns instead of words to represent where in their body they feel stress and anxiety.

When complete, identify which symptoms of stress cause the most trouble, such as aching muscles or worrying thoughts, and make a list of ways to counteract those symptoms, such as trying breathing techniques, using affirmation cards, etc.

Activity 6.7: Shrinking Worries

Resources required   *Worksheet 41: Shrinking Worries*
Activity aims   *To identify persistent worries and concerns*
   To reframe worries and to challenge the likelihood of them coming true

Worrying can be an exhausting and fruitless habit, created by unresourceful patterns of thinking and 'catastrophizing' – thinking the absolute worst will happen. Young people who persistently worry may notice an effect on their physical and emotional well-being.

While a young person may have legitimate issues or life problems to be concerned about, worrying doesn't actually achieve anything, and often blows a problem out of all proportion. A small worry can quickly escalate to an overwhelming anxiety.

Using Worksheet 41: Shrinking Worries, encourage the young person to identify his main worries or concerns and to write them on one side of the scale. Next, he should identify how realistic the worry is, on a scale from 1–10, where '1' is not realistic at all, and '10' is totally realistic and likely to happen. This can help young people put their concerns into perspective.

When complete, spend some time discussing ways to manage these worries, and create some empowering thoughts or affirmations to use instead when worries creep into the young person's mind.

Things That Make Me Feel Good or Bad

Think about all the things in your life that leave you with a good or bad feeling. These might be people, situations, things you do, places, and so forth. There are no right or wrong answers.

Things That Make Me Feel Good:	Things That Make Me Feel Bad:

Worksheet 38
Positive Thoughts

Thinking positive thoughts helps to keep our minds healthy. Sometimes when we feel angry or upset with someone, our thoughts can become so negative they take over other parts of our life.

Name some people in your life and think of a positive thought you can send them, for example, your parents, friends, classmates, teachers, etc. You might like to think about what you could say to the person, or what the person might need to hear. Start with a positive thought that you might need yourself!

Name of person	Positive thought I can send to them
You!	

Affirmation Cards

I am a valuable person	I have something important to contribute to the world
I am good company for others	Life is fun and enjoyable
I can be whoever I want to be	I am warm and kind hearted
I am a good person to know	I treat people with warmth and respect
I am likeable and liked	I have many gifts and talents to share

I am special and unique	Other people want to be around me
Life is a game, and can be fun	I am in control of how I feel
I am trustworthy	I care about others
I can choose what to think about and focus on	I forgive myself for any mistakes I make
My focus is on the present moment	I believe in myself
I am relaxed and at ease	I am proud to be who I am

Address the Stress

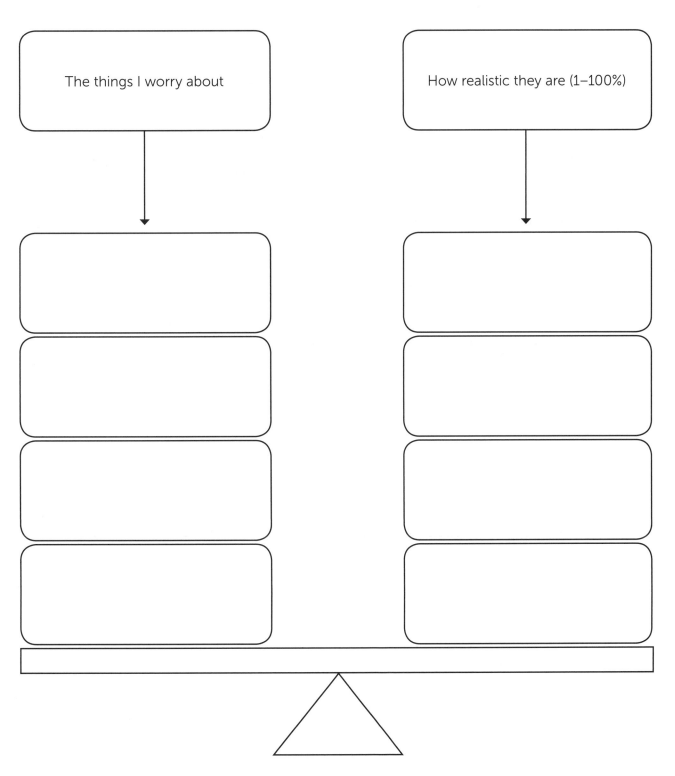

The things I worry about

How realistic they are (1–100%)

✓

Coaching Feedback Form

Name: _____

School: _____

Date: _____

Think about your time in coaching and take a few minutes to answer the questions below. There are no right or wrong answers. The ratings are as follows:

1: Totally disagree   **2: Disagree**   **3: Maybe**   **4: Agree**   **5: Totally agree**

1. Coaching sessions have helped me:

    1   2   3   4   5

2. I learned something about myself in coaching:

    1   2   3   4   5

3. Coaching has helped me to set and reach goals:

    1   2   3   4   5

4. I now have a clearer idea of how to help myself in the future:

    1   2   3   4   5

5. I would recommend coaching to someone else:

    1   2   3   4   5

6. Any additional comments?

Thank you for your time!

References

Akinbami, L., Liu, X., Pastor, P. and Reuben, C. (2011) *Attention Deficit Hyperactivity Disorder Among Children Aged 5–17 Years in the United States, 1998–2009*. Hattsville, MD: National Center for Health Statistics.

BACP (British Association for Counselling and Psychotherapy) (2007) *Counselling in Schools: A Research Study into Services for Children and Young People*. Lutterworth: BACP.

Cassells, R., Gong, H. and Duncan, A. (2011) *Race Against Time: How Australians Spend Their Time*. Sydney, Australia: AMP.

CDC (Centers for Disease Control and Prevention) (2011) *Youth Risk Behavior Surveillance System: 2011 National Overview*. Atlanta, GA: CDC. Available at www.cdc.gov/healthyyouth/yrbs/factsheets/index.htm, accessed on 4 June 2013.

CDC (2012) *Suicide Prevention*. Atlanta, GA: CDC. Available at www.cdc.gov/violenceprevention/pub/youth_suicide.html, accessed on 1 August 2013.

ChildLine (2012) *Saying the Unsayable: What's Affecting Children in 2012*. London: National Society for the Prevention of Cruelty to Children. Available at www.nspcc.org.uk/news-and-views/our-news/child-protection-news/12-12-04-childline-report/saying-the-unsayable-pdf_wdf93130.pdf, accessed on 25 July 2013.

Children's Society, The (2013) *The Good Childhood Report 2013*. London: The Children's Society. Available at www.childrenssociety.org.uk/news-views/our-blog/try-our-dynamic-good-childhood-report-2013, accessed on 31 July 2013.

Coaching Academy, The (2011) *National Occupational Standards in Coaching and Mentoring*. London: The Coaching Academy. Available at www.coachingacademyblog.com/national-occupational-standards-in-coaching-and-mentoring/#.UXGFicpPHo8, accessed on 19 April 2013.

DCSF (Department for Children, Schools and Families) (2007) *Children and Young People Today: Evidence to Support the Development of the Children's Plan*. London: DCSF. Available at http://dera.ioe.ac.uk/6957/1/7343-DCSF-Young%20People%20Today.pdf, accessed on 5 May 2013.

DfE (Department for Education) (2010) *Social and Emotional Aspects of Learning (SEAL) Programme in Secondary Schools: National Evaluation*. London: DfE. Available at www.education.gov.uk/publications/eOrderingDownload/DFE-RR049.pdf, accessed on 25 July 2013.

DfE (2012) *Children with Special Educational Needs: An Analysis – 2012*. London: DfE.

Dilts, R. (1980) *Neuro-Linguistic Programming: Volume I: The Study of the Structure of Subjective Experience*. Capitola, CA: Meta Publications.

Durlak, J., Dymnicki, A., Taylor, R., Weissberg, R. and Schellinger, K. (2011) 'Impact of enhancing students' Social and Emotional Learning: A meta-analysis of school-based universal interventions.' *Child Development 82*, 1, 405–432.

FCD (Foundation for Child Development) (2012) *2012 Child Well-being Index (CWI)*. New York: FCD. Available at http://fcd-us.org/resources/2012-child-well-being-index-cwi#node-1314, accessed on 19 July 2013.

Federal Interagency Forum on Child and Family Statistics (2013) *America's Children: Key National Indicators of Well-being, 2013*. Washington, DC: US Government Printing Office. Available at http://childstats.gov/americaschildren, accessed on 23 July 2013.

FPI (Family and Parenting Institute) (2012) *The Family Report Card 2012*. London: FPI.

Gingerich, W. and Eisengart, S. (2000) 'Solution-focused brief therapy: A review of the outcome research.' *Family Process 39*, 4, 477–498.

Goleman, D. (1996) *Emotional Intelligence: Why It Can Matter More than IQ*. London: Bantam Books.

Green, H., McGinnity, A., Meltzer, H., Ford, T. and Goodman, R. (2005) *Mental Health of Children and Young People in Great Britain, 2004*. London: Palgrave.

Herrera, V. and McCloskey, L. (2001) 'Gender differentials in the risk for delinquency among youth exposed to family violence.' *Child Abuse and Neglect 25*, 8, 1037–1051.

ICF (International Coach Federation) (2013) *What Is Professional Coaching?* Lexington, KY: International Coach Federation. Available at http://coachfederation.org/need/landing.cfm?ItemNumber=978&navItemNumber=567, accessed on 18 April 2013.

Ipsos MORI (2011) *Children's Well-being in the UK, Sweden and Spain: The Role of Inequality and Materialism.* London: Ipsos MORI. Available at www.unicef.org.uk/Latest/Publications/Ipsos-MORI-child-well-being, accessed on 31 March 2013.

Kernic, M., Wol, M., Holt, V., McKnight, B., Huebner, C. and Rivara, F. (2003) 'Behavioral problems among children whose mothers are abused by an intimate partner.' *Child Abuse and Neglect 27*, 11, 1231–1246.

Kim, J. and Franklin, C. (2009) 'Solution-focused brief therapy in schools: a review of the outcome literature.' *Children and Youth Services Review 31*, 4, 464–470.

Mattingly, M. and Bianchi, S. (2003) 'Gender difference in the quantity and quality of free time: The US experience.' *Social Forbes 81*, 3, 999–1030.

Miller, S., Hubble, M. and Duncan, B. (eds) (1996) *Handbook of Solution-focused Brief Therapy.* San Francisco, CA: Jossey-Bass.

O'Kearney, R., Anstey, K., von Sanden, C. and Hunt, A. (2010) *Behavioural and Cognitive Behavioural Therapy for Obsessive Compulsive Disorder in Children and Adolescents.* Hoboken, NJ: John Wiley & Sons.

Pew Research Center (2013) *Modern Parenthood Roles of Moms and Dads Converge as They Balance Work and Family.* Washington, DC: Pew Research Center.

Seligman, M. (1991) *Learned Optimism: How to Change Your Mind and Your Life.* New York: Knopf.

Seligman, M. (1995) *The Optimistic Child: A Proven Program to Safeguard Children Against Depression and Build Lifelong Resilience.* New York: Houghton Mifflin.

Stalker, C., Levene, J. and Coady, N. (1999) 'Solution-focused brief therapy: One model fits all?' *Families in Society 80*, 5, 468–477.

Stallard, P., Simpson, N., Anderson, S., Hibbert, S. and Osborn, C. (2007) 'The FRIENDS Emotional Health Programme: Initial findings from a school-based project.' *Child and Adolescent Mental Health 12*, 1, 32–37.

TECF (The Executive Coaching Forum) (2008) *The Executive Coaching Handbook: Principles and Guidelines for a Successful Coaching Partnership.* Boston: The Executive Coaching Forum.

UNICEF (United Nations Children's Fund) (2006) *Behind Closed Doors: The Impact of Domestic Violence on Children.* New York: UNICEF. Available at www.unicef.org/protection/files/BehindClosedDoors.pdf, accessed on 30 July 2013.

UNICEF (2013) *Child Well-being in Rich Countries: A Comparative Overview.* Innocenti Report Card 11. Florence: UNICEF. Available at www.unicef-irc.org/publications/683, accessed on 31 March 2013.

University of Southern California Annenberg School Center for the Digital Future (2013) *The 2013 Digital Future Report: Surveying the Digital Future.* Los Angeles, CA: University of Southern California.

Watanabe, N., Hunot, V., Omori, I.M., Churchill, R. and Furukawa, T.A. (2007) 'Psychotherapy for depression among children and adolescents: a systematic review.' *Acta Psychiatrica Scandinavica 116*, 2, 84–95.

Welsh Government (2011) *2011 Children and Young People's Wellbeing Monitor for Wales.* Cardiff: Welsh Government. Available at http://wales.gov.uk/about/aboutresearch/social/latestresearch/cypwellbeingmonitor/?lang=en, accessed on 26 July 2013.

Zins, J., Bloodworth, M., Weissberg, R. and Walberg, H. (eds) (2004) *Building Academic Success on Social and Emotional Learning: What Does the Research Say?* New York: Teachers College Press.

Index